EYE ON
Art

DISCARD

CLAUDE MONET

by Stuart A. Kallen

Cranton Area Schools
~~North Main Street~~
Granton, WI 54436

LUCENT BOOKS
A part of Gale, Cengage Learning

GALE
CENGAGE Learning

Detroit • New York • San Francisco • New Haven, Conn • Waterville, Maine • London

© 2009 Gale, Cengage Learning

LIBRARY OF CONGRESS CATALOGING-IN-PUBLICATION DATA

Kallen, Stuart A., 1955–
    Claude Monet / by Stuart A. Kallen.
        p. cm. — (Eye on art)
    Includes bibliographical references and index.
    ISBN 978-1-4205-0074-5 (hardcover)
    1. Monet, Claude, 1840–1926—Juvenile literature. 2. Painters—
France—Biography—Juvenile literature. 3. Impressionism (Art)—
France—Juvenile literature. I. Title.
        ND553.M7K35 2009
        759.4—dc22
        [B]
                                                                    2008020640

Lucent Books
27500 Drake Rd
Farmington Hills, MI 48331

ISBN-13: 978-1-4205-0074-5
ISBN-10: 1-4205-0074-0

Printed in the United States of America
1 2 3 4 5 6 7 12 11 10 09 08

CONTENTS

Foreword

"Art has no other purpose than to brush aside . . . everything that veils reality from us in order to bring us face to face with reality itself."

—French philosopher Henri-Louis Bergson

Some thirty-one thousand years ago, early humans painted strikingly sophisticated images of horses, bison, rhinoceroses, bears, and other animals on the walls of a cave in southern France. The meaning of these elaborate pictures is unknown, although some experts speculate that they held ceremonial significance. Regardless of their intended purpose, the Chauvet-Pont-d'Arc cave paintings represent some of the first known expressions of the artistic impulse.

From the Paleolithic era to the present day, human beings have continued to create works of visual art. Artists have developed painting, drawing, sculpture, engraving, and many other techniques to produce visual representations of landscapes, the human form, religious and historical events, and countless other subjects. The artistic impulse also finds expression in glass, jewelry, and new forms inspired by new technology. Indeed, judging by humanity's prolific artistic output throughout history, one must conclude that the compulsion to produce art is an inherent aspect of being human, and the results are among humanity's greatest cultural achievements: masterpieces such as the architectural marvels of ancient Greece, Michelangelo's perfectly rendered statue *David*, Vincent van Gogh's visionary painting *Starry Night*, and endless other treasures.

The creative impulse serves many purposes for society. At its most basic level, art is a form of entertainment or the means for a satisfying or pleasant aesthetic experience. But art's true power lies not in its potential to entertain and delight but in its ability to enlighten, to reveal the truth, and by doing so to uplift the human spirit and transform the human race.

One of the primary functions of art has been to serve religion. For most of Western history, for example, artists were paid by the church to produce works with religious themes and subjects. Art was thus a tool to help human beings transcend mundane, secular reality and achieve spiritual enlightenment. One of the best-known, and largest-scale, examples of Christian religious art is the Sistine Chapel in the Vatican in Rome. In 1508 Pope Julius II commissioned Italian Renaissance artist Michelangelo to paint the chapel's vaulted ceiling, an area of 640 square yards (535 sq. m). Michelangelo spent four years on scaffolding, his neck craned, creating a panoramic fresco of some three hundred human figures. His paintings depict Old Testament prophets and heroes, sibyls of Greek mythology, and nine scenes from the Book of Genesis, including the Creation of Adam, the Fall of Adam and Eve from the Garden of Eden, and the Flood. The ceiling of the Sistine Chapel is considered one of the greatest works of Western art and has inspired the awe of countless Christian pilgrims and other religious seekers. As eighteenth-century German poet and author Johann Wolfgang von Goethe wrote, "Until you have seen this Sistine Chapel, you can have no adequate conception of what man is capable of."

In addition to inspiring religious fervor, art can serve as a force for social change. Artists are among the visionaries of any culture. As such, they often perceive injustice and wrongdoing and confront others by reflecting what they see in their work. One classic example of art as social commentary was created in May 1937, during the brutal Spanish civil war. On May 1 Spanish artist Pablo Picasso learned of the recent attack on the small Basque village of Guernica by German airplanes allied with fascist forces led by Francisco Franco. The German pilots had used the village for target practice, a three-hour bombing that killed sixteen hundred civilians. Picasso, living in Paris, channeled his outrage over the massacre into his painting *Guernica,* a black, white, and gray mural that depicts dismembered animals and fractured human figures whose faces are contorted in agonized expressions. Initially, critics and the public condemned the painting as an incoherent hodgepodge, but the work soon came to be seen as a powerful antiwar statement and remains an iconic symbol of the violence and terror that dominated world events during the remainder of the twentieth century.

The impulse to create art—whether painting animals with crude pigments on a cave wall, sculpting a human form from marble, or commemorating human tragedy in a mural—thus serves many purposes. It offers an entertaining diversion, nourishes the imagination and the spirit, decorates and beautifies the world, and chronicles the age. But underlying all these functions is the desire to reveal that which is obscure—to illuminate, clarify, and perhaps ennoble. As Picasso himself stated, "The purpose of art is washing the dust of daily life off our souls."

The Eye on Art series is intended to assist readers in understanding the various roles of art in society. Each volume offers an in-depth exploration of a major artistic movement, medium, figure, or profession. All books in the series are beautifully illustrated with full-color photographs and diagrams. Riveting narrative, clear technical explanation, informative sidebars, fully documented quotes, a bibliography, and a thorough index all provide excellent starting points for research and discussion. With these features, the Eye on Art series is a useful introduction to the world of art—a world that can offer both insight and inspiration.

Introduction

Master of Impressionism

When Claude Monet went for a walk in the woods or a stroll along a beach, he glanced here and there like most people do. He gathered impressions of the landscape but rarely looked closely at the fine details of the scene before him. Unlike most people, however, Monet had the skill, talent, and creative drive to put these fleeting glimpses, or impressions, on canvas with brush and paint. Monet summed up his way of seeing while giving advice to an artist friend: "When you go out to paint, try to forget what objects you have before you, a tree, a house, a field or whatever . . . merely think here is a little square of blue, here is an oblong of pink, here is a streak of yellow, and paint it just as it looks to you, the exact color and shape, until it gives you your own naïve impression of the scene before you."[1]

Monet's painting technique came to be called Impressionism. He was the leader of this revolutionary style which was also practiced by renowned artists such as Édouard Manet, Paul Cézanne, Edgar Degas, Camille Pissarro, and Pierre-Auguste Renoir. The name Impressionism was invented in 1874 by a critic who wrote a review of Monet paintings at an exhibition.

Until Monet was forty years old, however, his talent for capturing momentary impressions on canvas with quick, flickering brushstrokes was widely treated with derision and disapproval by those in the elite world of French art.

Today, Claude Monet's works are sold for tens of millions of dollars. For most of his life, however, the artist struggled financially and was beset with many personal problems. He had a disapproving father, a sick wife, and lost a close friend and

Claude Monet was a revolutionary leader of the Impressionist movement.

patron in a senseless war. He also struggled in his career as the style he pioneered and loved so much went in and out of fashion as tastes changed and new artists gained favor with the critics.

Despite many setbacks in his personal and professional life, however, Monet continued to place strong demands on himself. He never stopped believing in the power of art to express ideas and transform the spirit. This may be confirmed by Monet's incredible output of more than twenty-five hundred paintings that radically altered the way art was understood and created.

Monet abandoned the studio to work *en plein air*, or in the open air. He took joy in painting outside, even during howling storms on the French coast or in snowy subzero temperatures in Norway. Casting aside the formal painting methods of earlier artists, Monet created art *sur le motif*, or on the spot. By doing so, he invented a unique way of viewing nature as a spontaneous, transient world of ever-changing light and color. As curator and leading Impressionist scholar Charles F. Stuckey explains, "[Monet] specialized in paintings of uncommonly brilliant light, in which physical objects dematerialize into fantasies. These works extend the original goals of Impressionism from [ordinary] pictorial journalism to meditative nature poetry."[2] Monet referred to these images as *féerique*, or fairy-tale-like.

During the second half of Monet's life, audiences finally recognized his genius. He was celebrated by the French people. Today, his home and gardens in Giverny, where he created so many of his paintings, are a national monument. It is listed among such famous French landmarks as the Eiffel Tower and the Arc de Triumph in tour guides. The main street running through Giverny is named Rue Claude Monet.

Long before he could dream of such honors, Monet's painting *Impression, Sunrise* gave a name to the most important artistic revolution of the nineteenth century. In the twentieth century his work influenced artists who painted styles such as cubism, surrealism, and abstract expressionism. Thus, Monet laid the foundations for modern art while creating unmatched visions of beauty that are among some of the most popular fine art images in the world today.

The Early Years

Oscar-Claude Monet was born in Paris on November 14, 1840. But his earliest memories were of the city of Le Havre, on France's northern Normandy Coast. Claude moved there with his parents, Claude-Adolphe and Louise-Justine Aubrée Monet, when he was just five years old. Historical accounts describe Le Havre as "born of the sea . . . the entire city lives by the sea and for the sea."[3] The watery environment of Le Havre inspired Oscar-Claude, who would become the city's most famous resident. He grew up painting his visions of the sea as well as those of the Seine Estuary, the winding River Seine, and Le Havre's beaches.

The Monets relocated to the busy port city to work in the wholesale grocery and ship chandlers' business owned by Claude's aunt Marie-Jeanne Lecadre and her husband. As chandlers, or merchants who sold groceries and provisions to shipping companies, the Lecadres were prosperous. They lived in a large villa facing the sea and often held parties and concerts for their large circle of friends.

After moving to Le Havre, Claude's father bought a big house in the business district next to the harbor. Claude grew up within view of large resort hotels, a beautiful beach, and a bay where hundreds of sailboats skimmed the waters. Many years later, Monet immortalized his parents' comfortable life in the 1886 painting *Terrace at the Seaside*. It depicts his father Claude-Adolphe seated in a beautiful garden, gazing out to sea while ships sail by and flags flutter in the breeze.

"I Would Have Been a Millionaire"

Despite the nostalgia portrayed in *Terrace at the Seaside*, Monet's father and uncles were conservative businessmen who hated the arts and had little use for painters. They encouraged young Claude to ignore his artistic side and instead study business. However, Claude had an intense dislike of school, which he called prison. He ignored his lessons in Latin, Greek, grammar, and math and spent his days doodling, drawing cartoons of his teachers in his notebooks. Monet was more interested in the art and drawing lessons he received from Jacques-François Orchard who himself had been a student of the famed French painter Jacques-Louis David. As soon as the school day ended, however, Claude escaped to the nearby beaches, cliffs, and ocean waters. He later recalled that as a child he thought, "I should like to be always near [the sea] or on it . . . and when I die, to be buried in a buoy."[4]

Little else is known about Monet's early life until his artistic career began in 1856. At the age of sixteen he began sketching charcoal caricatures, cartoonlike drawings of local dignitaries and tourists dressed in their best vacation clothes. Pictures such as *Léon Manchon, Notary* are typical of Monet's style at the time. The notary has an oversized head, a huge nose, exaggerated sideburns curling down his chest, sticklike legs, and miniscule feet.

The sketches were so inventive, humorous, and expertly drawn that they caught the eye of a local merchant who sold art supplies in a shop called Gravier's, located on Le Havre's fashionable Paris Street. Every Sunday morning Gravier's placed a new batch of Claude's drawings in the shop window where appreciative crowds gathered to see who the young

artist was mocking that week. The cartoons quickly sold for fifteen to twenty francs each, giving the sixteen-year-old artist a weekly income of about five hundred dollars in today's dollars —a sum equal to his schoolteacher's salary. "Had I carried on," Monet later remarked, "I would have been a millionaire."[5]

Monet grew up with his parents near the water and portrayed his parents' life in the painting *Terrace at the Seaside*.

Learning to Paint en Plein Air

Claude's caricatures were often displayed in Gravier's window alongside moody seascape and landscape paintings by Louis Eugène Boudin, a thirty-two-year-old artist who occasionally worked at the shop. Boudin painted outdoors, what the French called "en plein air," or in the open air. He believed that canvases

MONET GAVE COURAGE TO US ALL

Monet was known for his sometimes overbearing personality, even at an early age, as William C. Seitz writes in Claude Monet:

Most of the traits that were to make Monet a great painter were manifested early. . . . [He] was not religious—indeed, he had little faith in anything that was not drawn from direct experience. He was persistent, had small need for social approval, and was stimulated by both hostility and adversity: "Without my dear Monet, who gave courage to all of us," [Impressionist artist Pierre-Auguste] Renoir once recalled, "we would have given up!" But not all his traits were equally admirable. . . . Though willing to endure any degree of discomfort for his art, Monet was never to lose a taste for the overindulgent pattern of French middle-class life. He ate, it is said, like four men; he could be taciturn [reserved] and snappish, had a tendency toward vindictiveness, and exhibited a shameless craftiness where money and the sale of pictures were concerned. By the time he was sixteen he showed unmistakable talent, but he turned it to making caricature portraits at twenty francs a sitting.

William C. Seitz, *Claude Monet*. New York: Harry N. Abrams, 1982, p. 11.

Monet's personality became apparent at an early age.

produced in the open air had a power and energy that could not be matched by images created in a studio.

At the time, the idea of painting outdoors was a relatively new concept, made easy and convenient by various artistic innovations in the mid-nineteenth century. In earlier years, painters had to create their own pigments from minerals, plants, and animal parts, and mix them with oils in a studio environment. In 1800, however, bright new oil paints were sold in portable tin tubes for the first time. These paints were easy to use outdoors and were eagerly adopted by painters throughout Europe and the United States. The paints were packed with brushes and palettes into another recent innovation called the French easel. This was a versatile wooden box that held art supplies and opened up into a canvas holder which could be propped up anywhere, including beaches, riverbanks, fields, and forests.

Boudin took full advantage of such artistic advancements. After seeing Monet's expert caricatures, he convinced the young man to accompany him on a painting excursion to nearby Rouelles. Upon seeing Boudin open his French easel and commence painting en plein air, Monet was deeply moved: "Suddenly a veil was torn away. I had understood—I had realized what painting could be. By the single example of this painter devoted to his art with such independence, my destiny as a painter was opened out to me."[6]

The first drawings Claude made on outings with Boudin were created between July and September 1856. They consist of forty-six pencil sketches of scenery, sailing vessels, and local fishermen, gardeners, and children. The subject matter is simple, but the quality of drawings such as *Normandy Cottage in Ingouville* reveal talents beyond those of the average young artist. During this period, Claude also worked in color, using crayons of powdered pigment called pastels to create village scenes and seascapes such as *View of Sainte-Adresse*. These works reveal that Claude was already a skilled artist by this time. The details and the distinct contrasts between shadows and light show a professional touch that he had obviously been nurturing for a number of years.

The Beauty of Nature

Early on, Claude chose to depict scenes in nature. This set him apart from many local artists who were painting the modern buildings, railroads, and bustling ports built during Le Havre's rapid expansion since 1840. Describing the area, French writer and critic Jules Janin said that Le Havre was "the industrial warehouse for the entire world [and] the crossroads of all industrial products . . . [with] few remarkable monuments . . . [and] the most beautiful sugar refineries [and] construction yards in the region."[7] While these monuments to production were within easy walking distance of Claude's home, the young artist chose to visit the fields, forests, and shores as yet untouched by the swift development. Writing in *Claude Monet: Life and Art*, professor and Monet scholar Paul Hayes Tucker explains:

> Monet's first efforts . . . were understandable antidotes to the developments of the day. . . . [They] were attempts to stem [stop] the march of progress and to remind everyone of what was being lost as the country experienced profound . . . change. They also were paeans [joyful songs] to the beauties of nature and to humans' continuous struggle to be one with that world.[8]

Monet's choice of subject matter was undoubtedly influenced by the Barbizon School of painting that was active at the time. The Barbizon School was not a learning institution but a group of people who shared a similar artistic philosophy and style. It was named for the rustic village of Barbizon near the wild and beautiful Fontainebleau Forest located about 40 miles (64km) from Paris.

The rural community attracted painters such as Jean-François Millet and Camille Flers who were inspired by Barbizon's natural fields and forests untouched by human hands. Barbizon art also had a political aspect as the painters portrayed farmers, hunters, gravediggers, and other workers going about their daily tasks. These paintings were meant to show the common person as someone worthy of admiration, as opposed to the politicians, nobility, and military leaders who were romanticized by France's most popular artists at the time.

The Barbizon painters later provided a strong influence for the Impressionists, but in the 1850s their art was a commercial failure. It was rejected by the influential Académie des Beaux-Arts (Academy of Fine Arts) which held an annual or biannual exhibition called the Salon. Any artist who hoped for success had to be accepted by the Salon and those who were not accepted often stopped painting. Some even committed suicide.

As outsiders, the Barbizon painters held their own small art shows and lived the lives of poor, struggling artists. It is impossible to say if Claude was aware of the hardships faced by this school of nature artists, but he began to spend less time painting in the open air in order to pursue commercial success with his caricatures. Between 1856 and 1859, the young artist created dozens of satirical drawings, about sixty of which still survive.

While other artists were busy painting the industrial side of Le Havre, Monet chose to depict nature scenes in his paintings.

Serious Training in Paris

In 1857 Claude's mother died. Her sister, whom Claude called Aunt Lecadre, took over the young man's care and upbringing. As an amateur artist herself, Lecadre encouraged Claude to continue painting, even as his father insisted he continue his schooling to become a businessman. After his final exams,

THE BARBIZON SCHOOL

Monet's early work was influenced by painters of the Barbizon School who depicted the natural landscapes around the Forest of Fontainebleau south of Paris. The "Seine-et-Marne" Web page describes the Barbizon artists whose work later inspired the Impressionists:

In historical terms, [the Barbizon School] relates to the 1830 generation of artists who faded from the scene around 1875, opening the way for the Impressionists. Most of these painters were landscape and wildlife artists . . . [who] decided to go and find Nature "on her own ground." . . . This new approach reflected the "back to nature" trend which had begun during the 18th century. . . . These artists studied nature for her own sake, in the open air, "from the subject," without [reference to] a historical or mythological subject which, up until then, had been the main focus in landscape painting. . . . Gone was the idea of creating an imaginary, idealized landscape in their studios . . . with the addition of historical figures. In its place came the idea of depicting outdoor emotions and feelings when actually in the midst of nature. This desire for concrete observation and the freedom to choose an unusual subject . . . brought them into conflict with the [traditional art world of Paris].

Comité Départemental du Tourisme de Seine-et-Marne, "Seine-et-Marne," 2007. www.tourism77.co.uk/heritage-culture-france/sites-of-interest/barbizon-impressionists/barbizon.htm.

however, Monet announced his intention to move to Paris and become a professional artist. Describing the attraction to the big city, Tucker writes: "As the cultural capital of Europe and the center of artistic production and exchange in France, Monet knew it was where he could get serious training and be able to see significant art in abundance."[9]

Lecadre knew several painters who exhibited at the Salon des Beaux-Arts, and she convinced Claude-Adolphe to allow his son to move to Paris. With a letter of introduction from Aunt Lecadre, Monet visited Barbizon landscape painter Constant Troyon, a family friend. After viewing Monet's work, Troyon made his recommendations. Monet should first attend the École des Beaux-Arts (School of Fine Arts), run by the Academy of Fine Arts, followed by a summer of painting en plein air in Le Havre, with a return to school in autumn. Lecadre and Claude-Adolphe agreed to provide a steady allowance as long as Monet followed Troyon's plan.

By the spring of 1859 Monet was in Paris, joyously exploring the sprawling art markets. Writing to Boudin, he excitedly described the landscape paintings by Troyon, Charles-François Daubigny, and Jean-Baptiste Camille Corot as beautiful, marvelous, and astonishing. The eighteen-year-old Monet also showed he had a perceptive eye when criticizing respected painters. He described a seascape by Eugène Isabey as "a horrible, huge picture," and a landscape by Jean-Louis Hamon as "a terrible thing. . . . It's hypocritical and pretentious. In a word he knows nothing about nature."[10]

Such brash sophisticated observations show Monet was not intimidated by the Parisian art world. He seemed eager to compete with older, established artists. The art Monet saw also made him appreciate Boudin's talents more. Monet repeatedly urged the Le Havre painter to join him in Paris, which he believed was in desperate need of a good seascape artist. Monet even attempted to sell Boudin's paintings to a small group of agents and collectors he had met. Some historians believe, however, that Monet was mainly using Boudin as a way to meet those who might buy his own artwork. Commenting on this aspect of Monet's personality, Tucker writes:

Monet was looking to get something for himself out of all of these efforts, [a] practice that . . . became standard. It was this kind of maneuvering that Monet practiced for decades. He was not necessarily the kind of person one would want for a friend. While helpful when pushed, he generally looked out for himself, often feeling he deserved whatever he could get. . . . In part this feeling may have been due to the talent he knew he possessed from the beginning. In part it may have been the result of his desire to maintain the good bourgeois [upper class] standards that he appeared to have enjoyed when growing up. . . . The feeling of being special may also have been due to his uncanny and unabashed ability to assess the market, size up its players, and figure out exactly where he and everyone else stood. It was as if he deserved a commission for these analytical powers which he exercised over and over again during the course of his career.[11]

"Working with Great Concentration"

In February 1860 Monet decided that the best place to pursue both his artistic and business-related interests would be from a small rented studio in Montmartre, a hilly district that was the artistic center of Paris. Rather than attend the respected École des Beaux-Arts, Monet chose the Académie Suisse, a much less formal art school run by painter Charles Suisse. Such small independent schools were places where students learned directly from established "masters," whose work had been accepted by the Salon. Most students attended these schools hoping to receive enough training to pass the difficult entrance exam into the École, but Monet was attracted to the easygoing atmosphere of the academy.

At the Suisse the schedules were flexible. No exams or formal critiques of student work were given, and the teachers were down-to-earth artists rather than arrogant professors like those found at the École. As author Sue Rose explains, the

Académie Suisse was a perfect setting for Monet, who had long been uncomfortable in academic settings:

> The studio was large, bare, well lit, with two windows, one overlooking the courtyard, the other looking out across the river. The walls were grimy with smoke, and completely empty except for the easels and the models' metal crossbar, with its ropes and nooses used [by the model to maintain his stance while holding the] most difficult poses. The students shouted across to one another, teased the model, and puffed on their pipes, sending smoke up to the ceiling. Monet, though outgoing and popular, studied contentiously, working with great concentration.[12]

The relaxed setting at the Suisse had attracted an earlier generation of rebellious artists, and the school's alumni included renowned painters such as Eugène Delacroix, Honoré

In 1860 Monet chose Montmartre, which was known as the artistic center of Paris, to pursue his artistic interests.

Daumier, and Gustave Courbet. During his year at the school, Monet befriended several students who would themselves become famous, including Impressionist painters Camille Pissarro, Jean-Baptiste Armand Guillaumin, and Paul Cézanne.

Although classes at the Suisse started at six A.M., and night classes lasted from seven to ten P.M., Monet maintained a busy schedule outside of school. He attended openings at the Salon and visited museums, galleries, and the studios of other artists. He also spent hours talking with Troyon, who advised him to draw constantly in order to hone his skills. The older artist pointed out that Monet could visit the renowned Louvre to make sketches of the museum's masterpieces, and he could also travel to the country to paint in the open air.

Year in the Military

In 1861 Monet was drafted into the military. At the time, wealthy men could buy their way out of the service, and Claude-Adolphe offered to pay for Monet's discharge on the condition he return to Le Havre and work in the family business. Monet refused and instead signed up for a five-year term in a glamorous cavalry division called Chasseurs d'Afrique, or Hunters of Africa. With dreams of finding adventure in Africa, Monet shipped out to Algeria. Within one year, however, he contracted typhoid fever and was sent home on extended sick leave.

Back in Le Havre, the twenty-two-year-old Monet painted incessantly. Meanwhile, Aunt Lecadre, always seeking to help her nephew, offered to buy him out of the army at a cost of three thousand francs, a large sum that could have supported a typical French family for a year. However, both Lecadre and Claude-Adolphe insisted that no more money would be forthcoming unless Monet returned to Paris to study with a recognized teacher. He consented and was soon back in Paris under the guardianship of painter Auguste Toulmouche, a friend of his aunt's who had recently won a medal for his work in the annual Salon exhibition.

Toulmouche studied Monet's paintings and recommended he study with Charles Gleyre. Like Charles Suisse, Gleyre ran

THE CELEBRATED SALON

In the 1860s Paris was at the center of the Western art world with at least twelve thousand artists working in the city. The only hope of financial success for most was to have their work exhibited at the Salon, an annual or semiannual exhibition controlled by the Académie des Beaux-Arts. In The Private Lives of the Impressionists, *English author Sue Rose describes the turbulent social milieu surrounding the Salon:*

During the first two weeks of May, some 3000 visitors crowded into the [Salon]. . . . Up until the last minute, horses and carts arrived, bearing vast canvases and colossal sculptures, the top decks of the [horse-drawn buses] were crowded with artists and weighed down by pictures. The celebrated artists sent canvases measuring ten or twelve by twenty feet. . . . The vast exhibition filled more than two dozen rooms, and the exhibit took up the equivalent of some eight miles of space. The walls were crammed four deep with paintings, hung by the jury in spaces selected according to perceived importance; to be "skyed" (hung near the ceiling) was regarded as the ultimate slight, since the work hung there could barely be seen.

For artists, the salon exhibition was crucial. . . . [In] the days before dealers and small galleries it was the only real way of exhibiting their work, establishing a reputation as an artist, and attracting the attention of the aristocratic patrons and collectors and museum purchasers.

Sue Rose, *The Private Lives of the Impressionists*. New York: HarperCollins, 2006, pp. 7–8.

a tolerant school and encouraged artists to express their individuality. During his eighteen months at the school, Monet befriended several students including Frédéric Bazille, the son of a wealthy doctor who was studying medicine as well as art. Bazille held Monet in great esteem and would help him out of financial difficulties for many years. Renoir was also a student at Gleyre's, and he, Bazille, Alfred Sisley, and Monet formed bonds of friendship that would last throughout their lives.

"High and Mighty Academic Traditions"

By 1864 Monet was finished with school and was pursuing life as a Parisian artist. He painted landscapes in the Fontainebleau Forest and traveled to the Normandy coast to paint seascapes with Bazille. Before long, the two men were sharing a studio, and both were preparing paintings to submit to the Salon in March 1865. Monet's canvases depicted two seascapes, one of the Seine estuary, the other a view of the coast near Sainte-Adresse, a small town near Le Havre.

The annual Salon exhibition was incredibly important in the art world. It was attended by some of the most influential artists and art buyers in the world, and it was the cause of great anxiety for thousands of French painters. As important as the Salon was, it was also traditional and old-fashioned. The judges of the Salon jury were famously unadventurous as Jim Lane explains on the Salon des Refusés Web page: "It would be hard to imagine a more conservative gaggle of immobile, stodgy, establishment, stick-in-the-mud hacks bent upon cementing their high and mighty academic traditions in the minds of the public and artists alike, or a group of so-called "art experts" in the press corps more dedicated to aiding and abetting this effort."[13]

This art establishment was merciless upon those who did not conform to its traditionalist ideas. For example, the 1863 Salon had been exceptionally brutal, rejecting the now-famous painting *Luncheon on the Grass* by Édouard Manet. The jury considered the depiction of a nude woman at a picnic to be

vulgar and thought Manet's use of sharply contrasting tones and colors too experimental. The jury also rejected innovative works by Bazille, Sisley, and others. This caused an uproar in the arts community that might be compared to a stolen political election in modern times. Monet was not part of the 1863 Salon, but it might have influenced his choice of paintings when he finally did submit in 1865. Although he was widely known for his brashness, *The Mouth of the Seine at Honfleur* and *La Ponte de la Hève at Low Tide* were formal seascapes with muted colors. Conservatively executed following traditional artistic rules of perspective and composition, the scenes are

Monet painted numerous landscapes and seascapes and he submitted two seascapes to the Salon exhibition in 1865.

well within the style typically chosen by the jury. However, art scholar and museum curator William C. Seitz writes, the paintings show artistic touches unique to Monet:

> [The] skies are cloud-filled and the atmospheric tone . . . is silvery. The hues are not brilliant, but the sparkle and movements of the shore are nevertheless captured by the spontaneity of the brushwork, which varies from one passage to another. The beaches are often built up of crisp touches [of the brush], or even dotted, for they are in fact not sandy but composed of sea-rounded pebbles in a [number] of tones. Monet's quick brush also adapted itself to the chop of open water, the pound of surf, or, heavily loaded [with paint], to banks of clouds.[14]

Monet painted his own version of Manet's *Luncheon on the Grass*. Although he never finished it, his painting is considered revolutionary for its time.

The Salon Accepts Monet's Paintings

Both of Monet's paintings were accepted by the Salon along with works by Manet, Renoir, Pissarro, and Sisley. For his part, Monet declined to capitalize on his success by creating more paintings in the same style. Instead he set out in a new direction, beginning work on his own version of Manet's *Luncheon on the Grass*, building a huge canvas 15 by 20 feet (4.5m by 6m), for the Salon of 1866.

Although Monet never finished the massive work, his treatment of the subject, a conventional scene of picnickers in a forest, is considered revolutionary. Unlike other paintings of the time, the picture has no storyline and no center that draws the eye to a dominant subject. Instead, it simply portrays the picnickers as part of their surroundings, arranged in a seemingly haphazard manner quite distinct from traditional rules of composition.

Monet also showed realistic touches unseen in paintings at the time, such as a woman touching her hair and another putting down a plate. In this manner, Monet captured a spontaneous moment, something that might be observed in the blink of an eye. And in doing so, he took the art of painting into a new direction that would someday be imitated by thousands of artists throughout the world.

The Struggling Artist Breaks Through

I n 1865 Monet experienced a major artistic victory when two of his paintings were chosen for the celebrated Salon exhibition. When it came time for him to enter paintings for the 1866 Salon, he once again chose two paintings he assumed would be accepted by the conservative jury. *The Road to Chailly* is a well-executed, if rather traditional, landscape that Monet painted in 1864 near the village of Fontainebleau.

The second canvas however, *Camille (The Woman in a Green Dress)*, was completed only four days before the Salon deadline and delivered at the last minute. The huge canvas, 7.5 feet by 5 feet (2.2m by 1.5m) was a life-size portrait of Camille Doncieux, Monet's mistress. It highlights the contrast between her green striped satin gown and her white skin as she turns away from the viewer, looking coyly over her shoulder. Commenting on the pose and the artist's treatment of the subject, Rose writes: "The 'finish' of the textures—silk and fur, skin and hair—and the delicacy of her long, pale fingers, made this [painting] the epitome of an acceptable work. This was how the bourgeois audience wanted to see their women in art."[15]

Both of Monet's submissions were accepted by the Salon, but *Camille* became one of the most discussed paintings at the exhibition. Positive reviews in the press followed, and an important Paris art dealer offered Monet new commissions while helping him sell several paintings made in previous years.

A Scandalous Affair

For Monet the 1866 Salon Exhibition was a triumph, but the achievement had a troubling aspect. Camille Doncieux was still in her teens when Monet immortalized her on canvas. She was attractive, intelligent, and came from a wealthy family. However, Camille and Monet began living together without getting married, which was considered scandalous, and both of their families cut off financial support. This created a major rift between Monet and his father since, in addition to cutting off his allowance, Claude-Adolphe refused to accept Camille as one of the family.

Women in the Garden

Monet's success at the Salon gave him some relief from his financial difficulties. In the summer of 1866 he painted another large canvas, 8 feet 4 inches (255cm) by 6 feet 7 inches (205cm). Intended for the 1867 Salon, *Les Femmes au Jardin*, or *Women in the Garden*, depicts four women in expensive dresses, all of them posed by Camille. (Monet had to rent the garments since he could not afford to buy them.) Like *Luncheon on the Grass*, the painting shows the women in natural poses, one smelling a bouquet,

Camille (The Woman in a Green Dress) was a life-size portrait of Monet's mistress, Camille Doncieux. Monet submitted the painting to the 1866 Salon exhibition.

Women in the Garden, which depicts four women in expensive dresses in a garden setting, was rejected for the 1867 Salon exhibition by conservative judges.

another picking flowers, and a third woman holding flowers on her lap. This picture was one of the largest ever created en plein air, and the canvas was so big that Monet had to dig a trench in the garden and lower the painting into it with cables and pulleys so he could work on the upper area.

Much to the artist's dismay, *Women in the Garden* was rejected by the conservative judges on the Salon jury. In her book *Monet,* Vanessa Potts describes why they did not think it was worthy of exhibition:

Monet was aiming to make two significant points with [this painting]. This large size of canvas was traditionally reserved for historical or religious paintings that carried a moral message for the viewer. By painting an unremarkable modern scene, Monet was declaring that these everyday moments, painted in a realistic manner, were just as important in the art world as esteemed historical or religious subjects. His second point was concerned with the spontaneity of art, and painting exactly what was in front of the artist. Instead of sketching the scene and then completing it in the studio, Monet painted the entire work in the open air.[16]

The Salon jury also disapproved of the manner in which Monet painted the leaves and foliage in the painting, using dots and patches of color rather than blending the colors together to create realistic detail. Monet further explored this type of stylized painting, which would later become the hallmark of Impressionism, in his next work, *Jeanne-Marguerite Lecadre in the Garden*.

Zola Appreciates Monet's Style

Although the Salon rejected *Women in the Garden*, the influential novelist Émile Zola believed the painting was Monet's greatest so far. Zola was enthusiastic of Monet's new direction and asked the artist to head a group he formed called Les Actualistes. The name meant that its members were actual or authentic. According to Zola, these are "people who try to penetrate the exact sense of things and [whose] works are alive because they have taken them from life and have painted them with all love that they have for modern subjects."[17]

Zola's words appeared in a Salon review published in *L'Événement*, a major Paris newspaper. After reading Zola's article, Bazille decided to buy *Women in the Garden* for the stunning amount of twenty-five hundred francs, equal to the annual salary of a French factory worker. Unfortunately, Monet could not feel the satisfaction of instant wealth because Bazille agreed to pay the artist only 50 francs a month for 50 months. Oftentimes, the money was not paid in a timely manner, and Monet was forced to write dozens of letters to Bazille pleading

The Most Terrible Torments

Monet wrote dozens of angry letters to his friend and benefactor Frédéric Bazille pleading for money. In the following letter, written in August 1867, Monet tells Bazille that he is so poor he has been forced to move back in with his father. This meant that the artist left Camille, who recently gave birth to their son Jean-Armand-Claude Monet, alone in Paris:

I'm going through the most terrible torments, I had to come back here [to Sainte-Adresse] not to upset the family and also because I didn't have enough money to stay in Paris while Camille was in labor. She has given birth to a big and beautiful boy and despite everything I feel that I love him, and it pains me to think of his mother having nothing to eat. I was able to borrow the strict minimum for the birth and my return here, but neither she nor I have a penny of our own.

It's all your fault, so hurry up and make amends and send me the money right away to Sainte-Adresse: as soon as you get my letter, send a word by telegraph as I am terribly worried.

Really, Bazille, there are things that cannot be put off until tomorrow. This is one of them and I'm waiting.

Claude Monet, *Monet by Himself*, ed. Richard Kendall. Boston: Bulfinch, 1989, p. 25.

poverty and begging for his money. A typical letter reads, "I'm really angry with you; I didn't think you would abandon me like this, it really is too bad. It's now almost a month since I asked you first [for my monthly payment]: since then . . . I've waited for the postman every day and it's the same. For the last time I'm asking you for this *favor*."[18]

At the time of the letter, Camille was in Paris, pregnant with Monet's child, but the impoverished artist was living at his aunt's house in Sainte-Adresse. Monet left Paris not only to save money but to beg his father to accept Camille and their child. Although Claude-Adolphe recently fathered a child with his mistress, he refused his son's request and coldly instructed Monet to abandon Camille if he expected financial support from the family. Meanwhile, Monet remained in Sainte-Adresse, leaving Camille with no food and no blanket, crib, or toys for his son Jean-Armand-Claude, born August 8, 1867. After the birth, Monet lied to his father saying the relationship was over, but the artist spent the next seven months

Monet's painting *The Jetty at Le Havre*, which shows windswept waves breaking over a seawall, was accepted by the 1868 Salon jury.

shuttling back and forth between Camille's small Paris apartment and Sainte-Adresse, only disappearing for short periods so Adolphe would not suspect his son's defiance.

Monet's art did not suffer while he was living this double life. Between the summer of 1867 and March 1868, the artist completed more than twenty medium-sized canvases along with two large paintings for entry into the Salon exhibition. One of the smaller paintings, *Terrace at Sainte-Adresse*, portrays Monet's aunt and father in their comfortable surroundings, looking out to the sea. Monet painted the scene from an upstairs room in his aunt's house and, once again, the subject matter was considered unconventional because the people in the scene were facing away from the viewer. Of the large paintings, *The Luncheon* was an indoor scene with several figures in odd, spontaneous poses. This unusual painting was rejected by the Salon jury but *The Jetty at Le Havre*, showing windswept waves breaking over a seawall, was accepted.

Success at the International Maritime Exhibition

Soon after the 1868 Salon exhibition, Monet returned to the Le Havre region to paint pier and shipping scenes for another important art show, the International Maritime Exhibition to be held in Le Havre in July 1868. In order to concentrate on his work, he moved with Camille and his son to an inn located in the small town of Bonnières-sur-Seine, about 25 miles (40km) north of Paris. Although Monet's living conditions at the cheap rooming house were squalid, the inn was located in a remote spot, accessible only by an aged ferry-boat. The countryside around the inn was beautiful, surrounded by green meadows, wildflowers, and butterflies.

In this pastoral setting Monet painted *The River*, depicting Camille sitting on a riverbank staring out over the water. According to French art critic and artist biographer Jean-Paul Crespelle in *Monet*, this is "probably the first painting that is totally Impressionist in spirit. All the elements are there: water, iridescence, reflections, pale colors, colored shadows and, above all, that atmosphere of euphoria that is the movement's hallmark."[19]

The euphoria in the painting stood in sharp contrast to Monet's real life. Unable to pay the bills at the inn, he was evicted after a few months. Monet had to find temporary shelter for Camille and his infant son while he went to Paris in a desperate effort to borrow money from creditors. In order to extract more funds from Bazille, Monet even made up a story about a feeble suicide attempt:

> I must have been born under an unlucky star. I've just been turned out, without a shirt to my back, from the inn where I was staying. . . . [My] family refuses to do anything more for me and I don't even know yet where I'll be sleeping tomorrow. . . . I was so upset yesterday that I was stupid enough to hurl myself into the water [of the Seine River]. Fortunately no harm was done.[20]

Historians say Monet was an excellent swimmer, and it is doubtful he could have killed himself in this manner.

Monet's mood improved considerably when five of his paintings were included in the Maritime Exhibition. One of them, a painting of the port of Le Havre which had been rejected by the Salon earlier in the year, won a silver medal. The surrounding publicity of the Le Havre exhibition had other benefits for the artist. He sold *Woman in a Green Dress* to French novelist Arsène Houssaye for eight hundred francs, and the writer promised upon his death to leave it to Paris's prestigious Musée du Luxembourg in Luxembourg Palace. In addition, Louis-Joachim Gaudibert, a wealthy collector in Le Havre, commissioned Monet to paint portraits of his wife and other family members.

Fleeting Happiness in Étretat

In October 1868 Monet moved his family to Étretat, a village on the Normandy coast. He seemed to find happiness in Étretat. Writing to Bazille, Monet states:

SHOWING THE FAMILIAR IN AN UNTRADITIONAL WAY

In the summer of 1870 Monet spent an extended vacation at the fashionable resort town of Trouville with his family, friend and mentor Louis Eugène Boudin, and Boudin's wife. Over the years Boudin had successfully marketed paintings of the resort, and Monet thought he might take advantage of the public's enthusiasm for canvases of the vacation spot. However, as often before, Monet refused to make commercial paintings and instead pursued his own distinctive style. In Monet, Vanessa Potts explains the singularity of the work On the Beach at Trouville:

[T]his] picture depicts both Camille and Boudin's wife on the beach. . . . Monet's choice of subject again reflects his desire to record modern scenes. He chose to show this familiar resort in an untraditional way. Firstly the viewer is thrust in very close to the two women. . . . The result is to make the viewer slightly uncomfortable, as if he were invading an intimate scene. This discomfort is furthered by the relationship between the two women. The central space between them is empty; neither woman acknowledges the presence of the other. Their features are not detailed so there is an air of anonymity about them. . . . In the background other tourists can be seen, also devoid of identifiable features. This, combined with the quick, heavy brushstrokes, adds to the spontaneity of the painting.

Vanessa Potts, *Monet*. Bath, England: Parragon, 2001, p. 50.

On the Beach at Trouville *shows Monet's distinct style.*

I'm surrounded here by all that I love. I spend my time out-of-doors on the [beach] when the weather's stormy or when the boats go out fishing; otherwise I go into the country, which is so lovely here that I perhaps find it even more agreeable in the winter than in summer; and naturally I'm working all the time, and I think this year I'm going to do some serious things. . . . I am enjoying the most perfect tranquility and . . . would like to stay this way forever in a peaceful corner of the countryside.[21]

Like so many other times in Monet's life, trouble quickly followed success. In late 1868 when the Maritime Exhibition closed, the artist's creditors seized his unsold paintings and auctioned them off to the highest bidder. Fortunately, Gaudibert was able to purchase the paintings and return them to the artist. Nevertheless, the incident caused Monet much anguish, causing him to destroy several paintings to keep them out of the hands of his creditors.

Monet's spirits brightened temporarily when he began planning his next submissions for the Salon in early 1869. Recalling the success of *The Jetty at Le Havre*, he began work on a seascape, *Fishing Boats in the Sea*. The artist also decided to submit a winter landscape, *The Magpie, Snow Effect, Outskirts of Honfleur*, painted in the countryside near Étretat.

The Magpie Masterpiece

Painted on a frigid late afternoon in the middle of winter, *The Magpie* depicts a snow-covered wicker fence, woven from tree branches. A tan barn sits in the background shrouded by snow-laden trees, while the blue and purple shadows of late afternoon give the scene a forlorn feeling. A lone magpie perches on a small ladder on the left side of the canvas. Like most of Monet's subjects at the time, the bird is facing away from the viewer. It is the only other creature—besides the painter—out on such a desolate afternoon. And like the painter, the magpie seems to be pondering the light of the distant sea reflected on the vast horizon.

In *Monet: His Life and Complete Works* Sophie Monneret calls *The Magpie* "one of Monet's absolute masterpieces."[22] The Salon disagreed, however, and rejected the painting along with *Fishing Boats in the Sea*. Monet felt this snub was a disaster. In a letter to Houssaye he wrote, "After this failure I can no longer claim to cope. . . . [That] fatal rejection has virtually taken the bread out of my mouth, and despite my extremely modest prices, dealers and art lovers are turning their backs on me. It is, above all, very depressing to see the lack of interest shown in an art object which has no market value."[23] Monet's self-pity was also tinged with jealousy. Paintings by Manet, Renoir, Degas, Pissarro, and Bazille had all been accepted by the Salon.

A bright spot during this period came from gallery owner Louis Latouche, who was intrigued by Monet's evolving style.

In *The Magpie*, Monet painted a wicker fence woven from tree branches with a magpie perched on a small ladder, facing away from the viewer.

ART'S COURAGEOUS SOLDIER

Monet was fascinated with the way winter light reflected off the snow and ice in the French countryside. Some of his greatest masterpieces, such as The Magpie, *were painted outdoors when temperatures plunged below zero. When art critic Léon Billot discovered Monet working in a frigid field, he described the scene for the newspaper* Journal de Havre:

It was during winter, after several snowy days . . . [and the] desire to see the countryside beneath its white shroud had led us across the fields. It was cold enough to split rocks. We glimpsed a little heater, then an easel, then a gentleman, swathed in three overcoats, with gloved hands, his face half-frozen. It was [Monsieur] Monet, studying an aspect of the snow. We must confess that this pleased us. Art has some courageous soldiers.

Léon Billot, "Fine Arts Exhibition," *Journal de Havre*, October 9, 1868. Quoted in Charles F. Stuckey, ed., *Monet: A Retrospective*. New York: Park Lane, p. 40.

When Latouche placed one of the artist's scenes from Sainte-Adresse in the window of his Paris gallery, the work attracted large crowds who excitedly discussed the new style of painting. This did little to help Monet's financial situation, however.

Poverty and Happiness in Saint-Michel

Monet realized that he needed to be closer to Paris to survive as an artist. In the spring of 1869, with funds borrowed from Gaudibert, Monet and his family moved to a small cottage in the rural community Saint-Michel in the hills above a popular

Seine resort about 9.5 miles (15.2km) west of Paris. Now Monet could easily travel by train to Paris, but his attempts to sell his paintings failed. Within months the artist's finances hit rock bottom. His friend Renoir, who was living with his parents in a nearby village, helped Monet by raiding his family's pantry to provide food for Camille and her baby. Even with this help, Renoir told Bazille, "At Monet's house . . . things are getting serious. They don't eat every day."[24]

History has shown, however, that Monet often exaggerated his poverty in order to extract funds from his benefactors. And despite Renoir's comments, Monet wrote to Bazille around the same time and asked for a cask of wine instead of the money he was owed.

Monet's painting, *La Grenouillère* depicts a peaceful summer day and is considered a classic example of early Impressionism.

Another hint that things were not as bad as they seemed may be seen in the artist's work during this period. From the time he arrived in Saint-Michel to the time he left for Paris a year later, Monet produced about twenty canvases that can only be described as joyful and serene. Several of them were created at the boating and swimming resort at nearby La Grenouillère. Sitting side by side, Renoir and Monet refined the language of Impressionism. Monet's *La Grenouillère* captures a moment in time, a quick glance at boats, bathers, well-dressed tourists, rippling waters, and a café on the Seine. The view from the shady shoreline conveys the impression of a lazy, blissful summer day. Monneret describes the details:

> In the foreground, calm and coolness. Empty boats await their customers; their gentle rocking tinges the waves with horizontal touches, white, ultramarine, and ocher. In the shadows of the floating café . . . the crimson reflection of the edge of the boat streaks the water. The closer we come to the islet, the closer the colors come together and, in the space reserved for the bathing, the values become lighter, accentuating the ripples. In the distance we can barely make out a few boats passing along the far bank and the almost stylized vegetation with shades that herald the end of summer. All the lines of the boats, the gangways, and the café converged on the islet. . . . The central tree casts its shadow towards the edge of the picture, the very spot where the painter must be standing.[25]

Today *La Grenouillère* is considered a classic example of early Impressionism, and the place where it was painted is permanently linked to Monet and Renoir. However, Monet submitted a similar painting he made at La Grenouillère to the Salon jury of 1870, and it was rejected. The Salon did accept another picture of the scene, *By the Water*, painted by Ferdinand Heilbuth, and the differences between this painting and Monet's could not be greater.

Heilbuth's work is painted in the formal style of the eighteenth century. Gracefully posed female figures stand like stationary dolls before a landscape rendered in muted colors with smooth, nearly invisible brushstrokes. By contrast, Monet's painting (subsequently destroyed in World War II) was completed with numerous spontaneous brushstrokes, showy colors, and broadly rendered subjects who seem to be moving in a blur of action.

While Monet was pioneering a new painting style, the rejection by the Salon was still painful. Canvases by Renoir, Bazille, and Pissarro had been accepted along with about three thousand other works, three times more than were shown in the Salon of 1865. Monet may have found it somewhat encouraging that his rejection caused an uproar in the art world and the decision to reject was not unanimous. Two of the judges quit in protest, and the issue was covered in the press when Houssaye wrote an article in the widely read magazine *L'Artiste*, praising Monet. Houssaye also wrote that he was indeed going to leave *Woman in a Green Dress* to the Musée de Luxembourg, an announcement meant to help increase the value of Monet's other paintings. Despite the kind words, Monet would not enter another painting in the Salon until 1880.

Tourists in Trouville

In June 1870 Monet finally decided to marry Camille after living with her off and on for four years. Cynics have speculated that the artist married her for her dowry, which at this time was twelve thousand francs. However, it was understood that the sum would not be paid until Camille's father died, and Monet only received twelve hundred francs. This money was used not for family needs but to buy paints, canvases, and other art supplies. What was left was used to take an extended honeymoon in Trouville, a picturesque town on the Normandy coast south of Le Havre on the Seine estuary. Monet was joined at the resort by his friend and mentor Boudin and Boudin's wife.

Trouville was famous for its long sandy beach that stretched along the English Channel. The area attracted French, British, and American tourists. The railroad that connected the town to Paris was finished in 1863, and by the time the Monets visited there in the summer of 1870, several large hotels, restaurants,

souvenir shops, casinos, and a boardwalk had been built along the sand. Hoping to make some money off the tourist trade, Monet settled into the Hôtel Tivoli, one of the less fashionable resorts in town. During the following months Monet painted pictures of the beach and scenes along the boardwalk in his own unique style, including *Camille on the Beach*, *On the Beach at Trouville*, and *The Hôtel des Roches-Noires*. As Tucker writes,

Monet painted *Camille on the Beach* in Trouville, a picturesque tourist town on the Normandy coast.

> These canvases are filled with crisp, clear light and are generally rendered with a remarkable freedom, so much so that in certain areas . . . the lightly primed canvas

is clearly visible [under the paint] contributing to the freshness of the image and its windblown seaside appeal. In fact, bits of sand are actually embedded in the surface of several of these paintings."[26]

Although Monet had been a struggling artist for ten years by the time he painted the Trouville canvases, he had not let adversity stand in the way of his creativity. While many painters simply gave up their brushes and canvases after repeated rejection by the Salon, Monet was driven by more than the desire for money or fame. His singular way of viewing light and image and his method of committing it to canvas were enough to keep him going through both good times and bad.

The Impression of Success at Argenteuil

The year that Monet celebrated his thirtieth birthday was the start of a difficult time in France. In July 1870 France declared war on Prussia and other states in present-day Germany, starting what is called the Franco-Prussian War. While Monet painted merry scenes of carefree tourists in Trouville, the Prussian military destroyed the French army in battle after battle. All able-bodied men, including Monet's artist friends, were expected to come to the defense of France. Bazille enlisted in the army in July 1870, Renoir was drafted into the cavalry in August, and Manet and Degas soon volunteered for the National Guard.

In late August the French suffered a bloody and humiliating defeat. By September 18 the Prussian army had surrounded Paris, forcing the population into a long period of starvation. On September 28 Monet was shocked to learn that Bazille had been killed in battle. He was not only a good friend but had been an important source of funds for nearly a decade.

The winds of war did not prevent Monet from continuing his quest to redefine painting. Looking at his canvases from that period, the viewer would not see a hint of the tragedies that were befalling his country. Nor is there any expression of the pain the artist must have felt in July when his Aunt Lecadre died. Instead, Monet continued to render spontaneous moments of ephemeral light captured in quick brushstrokes on the beach in Trouville. By October, however, Monet had to face the reality of war. The government had placed him in the reserves, and the artist feared he would be drafted. As a result he sneaked out of the Hôtel Tivoli in Trouville without paying his bill and fled to London with Camille and his son.

An Economic Windfall in London

By the time Monet arrived in London, the city was filling with French exiles, many of them artists or wealthy patrons of the arts. Among them was painter Charles-François Daubigny, an old friend of Monet's who introduced the artist to exiled art dealer Paul Durand-Ruel. Tucker describes the historic significance of this event: "[This] trip provided [Monet] with an economic windfall as Daubigny . . . insisted that Durand-Ruel purchase works from this up-and-coming artist. It was probably the most important introduction Monet ever received as Durand-Ruel soon became Monet's main conduit for selling pictures and his primary source of funds for more than three decades."[27]

Initially, Durand-Ruel purchased only one painting, *Break-water at Trouville, Low Tide*, but he chose to display the canvas at the opening of his new art gallery on London's fashionable Bond Street. Called the Annual Exhibitions of the Society of French Artists, this show was the first of ten annual events that displayed the work of French painters to a British audience.

Just as Londoners were learning about French art, Monet was able for the first time to study British painters firsthand. London's celebrated National Gallery exhibits dozens of works by renowned artists John Constable and J.M.W. Turner, neither of whom was shown in Paris. Monet was particularly inspired by Turner's seascapes and landscapes and the way in which the English artist rendered the effects of light. As John Piper writes in *British Romantic Artists*, Turner "painted *light*—veiled light, or misty light, or full light, or blinding light."[28]

Doubtlessly, Turner's paintings such as *Lausanne*, with its shimmering colors, intense contrasts, and barely recognizable subject, were closely studied by Monet. Of the six canvases Monet later painted in London, two scenes of the Thames River show the influence of *Lausanne*. Unlike his bright, cheery canvases of the Normandy Coast, however, *The Thames Below Westminster* and *Boats in the Port of London* describe the typical gloomy weather of the British winter. Perhaps these gray canvases suited the artist's mood since they were created around the time Monet's father died in Sainte-Adresse. While saddened by the death, Monet was also disappointed to learn that Claude-Adolphe left no inheritance for his son.

The Thames Below Westminster illustrates the gloom of a typical British winter.

Inspiration in Holland

By the time Monet left London in May 1871, the Franco-Prussian War was over. France lost the war, but the peace settlement stipulated that the Prussians were to leave Paris. Even so, the city remained in turmoil. An attempt by a large group of Socialists called the French Commune to seize control of the government was brutally repressed by the French military. Approximately thirty thousand so-called Communards were killed during a seven-day period in May now known as "Bloody Week." In the aftermath of the battle, Monet was incorrectly informed that his good friend, painter Gustave Courbet, was killed. This led Monet to speak out strongly against the French government. In reality, Courbet survived but was forced to spend four months in prison for his role in the Communard uprising.

So although the war was over, Monet was still fearful of returning to Paris. Instead, he went to Holland, using money from the first purchase of his paintings by Durand-Ruel. After traveling

Landscape at Zaandam was part of Monet's Holland series. During one summer in Holland, he painted twenty-four paintings.

by train through the country, he settled in early June in the small village of Zaandam, about 5 miles (8km) from Amsterdam. Holland, with its ancient windmills, vast tulip gardens, bucolic fields, and picturesque canals, strongly appealed to Monet.

The artist also appreciated the Dutch people, many of whom spoke perfect French and respected artists whether or not they were famous. Writing to Pissarro about his experiences, Monet stated that Holland "is much more beautiful than what they say . . . [and Zaandam has] houses of all colors, windmills by the hundreds, and enchanting boats. . . . There is enough to paint here for a lifetime."[29] During the summer in Holland, Monet produced twenty-four paintings, including *The Port of Zaandam, The Zaan at Zaandam*, and *Windmills Near Zaandam*. He also had his photograph taken by Amsterdam photographer A. Grenier. The picture shows a thoughtful Monet with his longish beard, peering somewhat suspiciously at the camera.

Continued Success in Argenteuil

Monet finally returned to Paris in the autumn of 1871. Many important public buildings, including the Tuileries Palace, the Palais Royal, and the Palais de Justice, lay in ruins. Typically, Monet's paintings did not reveal a hint of the destruction of his city nor the hardships suffered by his friends who witnessed mass famine and death. In fact, despite the depressing situation in Paris, Monet was beginning to enjoy the most successful years of his career thus far. Durand-Ruel was buying his paintings on a regular basis, and the dealer had cultivated a large base of wealthy customers who were interested in Monet's style.

In mid-November Monet rented a studio in Paris, which was mainly used as an office and storage space. In December he moved his family to a rented house in Argenteuil with a view of the Seine. The move to this scenic countryside town, which was then home to about eight thousand people, gave Monet easy access to Paris, about 9 miles (15km) to the south.

MONET'S HOME IN ARGENTEUIL

By early 1872 Monet's paintings were finally selling, and this provided him with enough money to move his family to an idyllic home in Argenteuil. The artist's life at the time is described by Sue Rose in The Private Lives of the Impressionists:

Monet's house was spacious, with parquet floors, French windows, and a ravishing country garden teeming with color in summer. He could stand on his lawn and watch the boats coming and going [on the Seine], and all the activity of the riverside. On sunny days, a table was spread with a glistening white cloth beneath the large horse-chestnut tree, and the family lunched out of doors, little Jean playing on the grass. Monet painted the scene, with Camille's hat hanging in the bough of the chestnut tree, its ribbon trailing from the branches. . . .

The spring of 1872 was fresh and radiant. Gardens and orchards seemed to bloom all at once. . . . Suddenly, there was enough money to buy a small boat. . . . Monet had a wooden cabin built on it and set it up as a small studio, just big enough to take his easel. Manet painted [Monet] in his studio boat, knees drawn up, hat brim turned down, floating on the river, absorbed in painting the water. Inside the house, Monet painted Camille through the French windows, framed by the open russet-colored shutters festooned with flowers. She wore pale pink and blue dresses that summer, with little white collars and pretty hats all decorated with flowers. In some paintings, posed against the banks of flowers, she seems to rise up from a haze of pulsating color.

Sue Rose, *The Private Lives of the Impressionists*. New York: HarperCollins, 2006, p. 100.

Argenteuil also attracted other painters including Manet, Boudin, Sisley, and Renoir. The wealth of artistic scenery, both pastoral and modern, is described by Paul Hayes Tucker in *The Impressionists at Argenteuil:*

> Argenteuil's appeal to the impressionists derived mostly from its diversity, which offered something for everyone. Depending on where one looked, the town could be charmingly historic or unnervingly progressive. Monet encountered these contrasts on a daily basis. Directly across the street from his house on the rue Pierre Guienne . . . stood an impressive eighteenth-century building that served as the town hospice. When he walked out his front door, he could see the newly renovated Boulevard Héloïse . . . and the promenade to the right. If he turned to his left, he could see the railroad station and several factories, beyond which stretched residential streets that led to the vineyards and the Orgemont hill with its windmill restaurant. Everything was within walking distance.[30]

With inspiration in every direction, not only was Monet producing more than ever, he also had in Durand-Ruel a willing buyer for his prolific output.

The art dealer's wife had died recently and, without her advice, Durand-Ruel was purchasing many more paintings than he could sell from Renoir, Sisley, Manet, and others. Monet, however, was the prime beneficiary of this situation. In 1872 the artist received 9,880 francs from Durand-Ruel for twenty-nine of his canvases. In addition, Monet sold another ten pictures for 2,220 francs, giving him an income that year of 12,000 francs. This was comparable to the salary of a French doctor and about six times more than the average earnings of typical workers in Argenteuil.

For the first time, Monet was able to live in the grand style he had desired for so long. He entertained other artists at his home and purchased a substantial quantity of wine to share with his guests. He hired two domestic servants and a gardener. He also bought a small boat which he converted into a floating art studio. Manet was so amused at the sight of

Monet used a small boat as a floating art studio and Manet was so amused by this that he immortalized the scene in *Claude Monet in His Studio Boat*.

his friend painting in the cramped little vessel that he immortalized the scene in *Claude Monet in His Studio Boat*. Monet also painted pictures of the watercraft docked along a tranquil stretch of the Seine in the picture *The Studio Boat*.

Painting "The Work-a-Day World"

During Monet's first year at Argenteuil, he produced sixty paintings. Several, such as *Camille Reading* and *Jean Monet on His Horse Tricycle*, included the artist's wife and son as subjects. Monet also created many paintings of everyday scenes around Argenteuil. These include *Houses by the Edge of the Fields*, showing new housing developments, and *Springtime in Argenteuil*, a pastoral riverbank scene nearly untouched by humanity. Monet depicts the leisurely pace of life along the river with stunning colors, dreamy cloud-filled skies, transitory shadows, and light that almost shimmers upon the canvas in *The Promenade at Argenteuil, The Basin at Argenteuil*, and *Pleasure Boats at Argenteuil*. These paintings were typical of Monet's subject matter.

In addition to everyday scenes around Argenteuil, Monet also painted scenes that showed the changes that war and industrialization had brought to Argenteuil. For example *The Highway Bridge Under Repair* shows the city's main bridge over the Seine which had been blown up during the war. Unlike

Jean Monet on His Horse Tricycle featured Monet's son, Jean, as the subject.

Monet and his friends, who were all Impressionist painters, worked together regularly at Argenteuil, oftentimes rendering the same subjects. Paul Hayes Tucker explains in The Impressionists at Argenteuil:

[It] might have been possible to mistake a canvas by Monet for one by Renoir . . . at Argenteuil. Time and again in the 1870s Monet stood side by side with one of his artist friends rendering the same scene: The Boulevard Héloïse, a regatta on the Seine, the boat basin with sailboats and [oars], the railroad bridge. . . . Sisley was first to join Monet in Argenteuil, and they initiated the custom. Monet and Renoir, the second to visit, soon followed suit. Manet worked beside Renoir once, both of them painting Monet's wife Camille and son Jean in Monet's backyard.

The impressionists also produced many pictures of each other during their stays with Monet. Renoir sketched or painted his host four times and Camille as many; Manet did two portraits of Monet painting in his studio boat with Camille by his side as well as one of the whole family; Monet painted at least one image of Manet in the garden. This habit not only deepened their friendships and avoided the expense of models, it encouraged them to support one another in the face of the challenges they had so ambitiously posed for themselves. In the process they were able to fulfill their equally important aim to base art on life, and as an added benefit, they could elevate themselves and their practice to a level of significance that affirmed their claims to history.

Paul Hayes Tucker, *The Impressionists at Argenteuil*. Washington, DC: National Gallery of Art, 2000, p. 23.

the picturesque subjects usually chosen by Monet, this painting is drab, utilizing browns, grays, olive greens, and muted blues to depict a forlorn mood. The dreary bridge is reflected in the water as the smoke from a factory rises into the distant sky. On top of the bridge, a horse-drawn carriage and a dozen silhouetted figures make their way along the span. Describing the painting, Tucker observes:

> This is not a place of reverie or retreat; it does not even fall into the category of the obviously "beautiful." Instead, this is the work-a-day world of daily jobs and commuting and anonymous encounters in repetitive situations. Tentative but determined, loosely painted but highly calculated, the scene suggests that some of the [tensions] of modern life are present even in those areas outside the city which many urban dwellers hoped were free of such strains. These tensions—between labor and leisure, familiarity and aloofness, the human and the natural—were particularly poignant [meaningful] for a nation emerging from the disasters of the previous year.[31]

Monet painted similar scenes when he produced twelve canvases during visits to Rouen, France, the capital city of Normandy. *The Train* depicts a locomotive, rendered with a series of quick dabs of black paint, steaming past dozens of factories blowing smoke from their stacks. Several tiny figures are dwarfed by the scene of industrialization and are facing away from the viewer. While these bleak views of progress were not typical Monet paintings, Durand-Ruel easily sold the canvases and asked Monet to produce more. Nineteenth-century art collectors viewed such paintings as proof that France was reemerging as a strong nation after the crushing defeat by the Prussians.

Impression, Sunrise

Monet's most iconic canvas of the era was not painted in Argenteuil. It was painted in the artist's hometown of Le Havre. Monet had created several sketches and paintings of Le Havre's inner harbor looking out the window of his room at the Hôtel de l'Amirauté at different times of day.

Impression, Sunrise was Monet's most iconic canvas of the era. The painting portrayed the harbor at Le Havre and the colors he used were both subdued and bold.

Originally called *Marine*, the painting *Impression, Sunrise* captures the harbor at a fleeting instant when the sun emerged from the mist, silhouetting vague shapes of ship masts and buildings in the distance. Although most of the canvas is painted in subdued tones of bluish lavender, green, and gray, the bright orange fire of the sun leaves a streak on the surface of the water and adds tones of pink, orange, and red to the dawn sky.

Monet probably painted *Impression, Sunrise* over the course of a few days in Le Havre, and it was only one of many canvases the artist was creating every month. By February 1873 Monet had produced enough such paintings to sell another twenty-five to Durand-Ruel for 12,100 francs. Pictures of four of Monet's paintings were published in the art dealer's voluminous catalog, and the preface to the edition was written by respected art critic Armand Silvestre. The critic pointed out for the first time that works by Monet, Sisley, and Pissaro were similar in style and that this group of artists was different from other contemporary painters because their harmonious approach was making a fresh impact on viewers. Silvestre stated that of this group, Monet was the most daring painter of his generation.

Japanese Influence in Monet's Work

Another observation stood out in Silvestre's preface. He noted that Monet's irregular brushstrokes were similar to those seen in Japanese images hand-printed from blocks of wood. Doubtlessly, Monet was influenced by Japanese prints. The artist had first seen such prints on wrapping paper in an Amsterdam food shop in 1871, and he was so taken with their beauty, he bought a Japanese engraving that was hanging on the wall. He went on to collect 231 of the prints.

Prints by nineteenth-century Japanese masters such as Katsushika Hokusai and Kitagawa Utamaro were extremely popular in Paris at that time. They featured flattened or tilted spaces, vibrant colors, no shadows, and unbalanced or asymmetrical compositions that did not follow traditional Western art standards. The Japanese artists emphasized small gestures in subjects or casual details and also had a profound reverence for nature. In discussing the influence of Japanese art on Monet, journalist Don Morrison writes in *Time*: "Printmaking is a more cumbersome and less forgiving process than painting, so Japanese artists developed a remarkable economy of expression. Utamaro, for instance, could with a mere line or two describe the course of a river. . . . Thus could Monet—in *Impression, Sunrise* . . . conjure up a boat with a mere squiggle of the brush."[32]

The Society of Painters, Sculptors, and Engravers

While Silvestre praised Monet's Japanese influences, the jurors at the Salon were less impressed. In 1873, fearing another rejection, Monet decided to shun the Salon and hold his own show with other Impressionists. This Exhibition of Independent

MONET AND JAPONISME

Monet was fascinated by Japanese art prints that became popular in France in the 1870s and 1880s. He collected more than 230 of the prints, and these works came to be extremely influential among Impressionist painters. The prints depicted landscapes such as Mount Fuji, historical tales, and battle scenes. They also focused on the urban Tokyo culture of beautiful geishas, actors in the Kabuki theater, pleasure houses, and high-class prostitutes. Hand-printed with wooden blocks, the inexpensive prints were known as ukiyo-e, or "images of the floating world." This phrase refers to the youth culture of Tokyo, so called because the youth were thought to be a society unto themselves, lost in their own floating world.

French artists such as Monet, Manet, and Pissarro became fascinated with ukiyo-e and other products of Japanese culture. This was part of a fad among artists and intellectuals called Japonisme, or love of the Japanese style. It was a result of Japan opening its long-isolated society to outsiders in the 1870s. As trade barriers fell, European department stores and art galleries were suddenly filled with ukiyo-e.

Monet never traveled to Japan. But because of his artistic eye, he only purchased the highest quality prints created by masters such as Utagawa Hiroshige, Katsushika Hokusai and Kitagawa Utamaro. This included rare battle scenes as well as Westerners relaxing in geisha houses in Yokohama.

Artists was the first held in Paris without government, commercial, or private financial support. The artists would sponsor themselves. After a series of meetings at Argenteuil with Pissarro, Degas, Renoir, Sisley, and others, the artists banded together to form the Society of Painters, Sculptors, and Engravers.

The First Exhibition of Independent Artists opened on April 15, 1874, in a gallery on the Boulevard des Capucines, the center of the Paris art world. The exhibit included 160 paintings representing twenty-nine artists. Monet displayed nine paintings, including *Impression, Sunrise*. During the one-month exhibit, the show received extensive coverage in Paris newspapers and was attended by about thirty-five hundred people. At least fifty art critics reviewed the show. Most reviews were favorable, and Jules Castagnary, writing in *Le Siècle*, described the term *Impressionist* for the first time in print:

> The consensus that unites [these painters] and makes them a collective force in our disintegrated age, is their determination not to seek an exact rendition but to stop at a general appearance. Once that impression is fixed, they declare that their part is played. . . . If we must characterize them with one explanatory word, we would have to coin a new term: Impressionists. They are Impressionists in that they render not the landscape but the sensation evoked by the landscape. The very word has entered their language: not *landscape* but *impressionism*, in the title given in the catalog for Monet's *[Impression,] Sunrise*. From this point of view, they have left reality behind for a realm of pure idealism.[33]

Several other reviews of the show were scathing. Writing in *La Presse*, Emile Cardon stated: "The scribblings of a child have a naiveté and sincerity that make you smile; the debaucheries of this school are nauseating and revolting."[34] The most famous review of the show, however, was a satire written by landscape artist Louis Leroy. His widely read lampoon in *Le Charivari* was responsible for popularizing the term *Impressionism*. In the piece, Leroy imagined the dialogue of an old-fashioned painter, Vincent, upon viewing *Impression, Sunrise:* "This one is Papa Vincent's favorite! . . . *Impression Sunrise. Impression*— I knew it. I was just saying to myself, if I'm impressed, there must be an impression in there. . . . Wallpaper in its embryonic state is more labored than this seascape."[35]

The Society of Painters, Sculptors, and Engravers did not use the term *Impressionism* until their third art show in 1877, which was called Exhibition of Impressionists. This was the only time the expression was officially used by the painters. It is likely that they did not want to be limited by the label.

Painting at an Amazing Pace

Monet's output of Impressionist painting continued at an amazing pace. Throughout the mid-1870s the artist continued to paint Argenteuil and the surrounding area including railroad and highway bridges, the view from his backyard, the promenade along the Seine, views from his studio boat, and summer regattas. While the subjects were similar, each painting was different, influenced by the clouds and shadows, the angle of the sun, the time of day, and the various seasons. Drawing on these inspirations, Monet produced forty canvases in the summer of 1874 alone.

Monet also continued to paint Camille and Jean in various poses, several of which are timeless classics that define the era. *Madame Monet and Her Son on the Hill* was hung at the Second Exhibition of Independent Artists in 1876. As Monneret writes:

> Camille is standing at the top of the hill which her son has not yet reached. . . . The small, hard, fast, stabbing touches [of Monet's brush] give the foreground of the meadow a kind of motion accentuated by the range of greens barely tinged by the yellow of a few small indecisive flowers. Longer touches swirl the clouds, which the wind seems to be shredding. It shakes [Camille's] sun shade, sweeps up the skirt, blows back the veil. Monet receives those visual sensations and transmits them to the viewer."[36]

Another painting of Camille, *La Japonaise (Camille Monet in Japanese Costume)*, clearly illustrates Monet's fascination with Japanese art. Camille poses in a long, red kimono, with an uncharacteristic smile, holding a Japanese fan to her face. Monet produced *La Japonaise* for the Second Exhibition of Independent Artists to show he could paint something other

than landscapes. The painting was the intense focus of Paris art critics. Many compared it positively to *Woman in a Green Dress*, Monet's triumph from the 1866 Salon. It is probable the artist was hoping for the same type of payoff from the new painting.

Hard Times Again

By this time the French economy had taken a downturn, and Durand-Ruel was no longer buying Monet's canvases. All the money the artist had made in previous years was gone, and once again he was writing letters to friends bitterly complaining about his economic circumstances. The town butcher and baker had stopped extending credit to Monet, and creditors were pounding on his door. He even implored Manet to send him twenty francs so he could buy a few days' food for his family.

By 1877 Monet had other problems in Argenteuil besides poverty. The town was growing rapidly, and a new iron foundry, a distillery, a chemical plant, and a new railroad line were producing clouds of air pollution that contaminated the shimmering light documented in Monet's earlier works. In addition, Paris officials had constructed a sewer line that was now dumping tons of raw sewage into the Seine. The stinking mess floated downriver to settle in Argenteuil's boat basin where Monet kept his studio boat.

Discouraged by these new developments, the artist temporarily moved to Paris in January 1878, and his second son, Michel, was born there on March 17. While the birth of his child cheered him, the artist's career began to flounder. In June one of Monet's art patrons, Ernest Hoschedé, filed for bankruptcy and was forced to sell his collection of sixteen Monet canvases. However, the artwork only attracted low bids, a reflection of the economic slump.

Tired of Argenteuil, in August 1878 Monet moved to Vétheuil, a small town north of the city. From this point onward, Monet would never again paint scenes of the city, the suburbs, factories, and bridges. Having lost his faith in progress and modernity due to the pollution of Argenteuil, the artist would focus solely on the beauties of nature and the iridescent light of the natural world.

Painting His Way into History

W hen Monet moved to Vétheuil in 1878, the town had six hundred residents and had not grown in centuries. It was about one-tenth the size of Argenteuil, where the artist had previously resided. And unlike Argenteuil, Vétheuil had no factories or housing developments—the town did not even have a rail line running through it to bring tourists from Paris. For six hundred francs a year, Monet was able to rent a house on a rural road and continue to pursue innovative art. During the three years he lived in Vétheuil, Monet was more prolific than ever, producing almost three hundred paintings, or one every four days. Even as his output of beautiful, joyous paintings continued at an impressive pace, his personal life took a turn for the worse.

Although he continued to sell his paintings, his expenses were high, and he was beleaguered by money problems, often without a franc to buy groceries. This caused frequent depression and great insecurity concerning his work since buyers did not seem to see the value of it. Writing to art collector Georges De Bellio in March 1879, Monet, then thirty-eight-years old, despairingly stated:

I am absolutely sickened with and demoralized by this life I've been leading for so long. When you reach my age, there is nothing more to look forward to. . . . Each day brings its tribulations and each day difficulties arise from which we can never be free. So I am giving up the struggle once and for all, abandoning all hope of success, and I no longer have the strength to work in such conditions. I hear that my friends are preparing another exhibition this year but I must discount the possibility of participating in it since I have nothing worth showing.[37]

Monet was often known to exaggerate his misery, but in the summer of 1879 the artist faced a real tragedy when his wife and muse Camille became gravely ill with cancer. For several months she was in horrible pain, prompting Monet to tell De Bellio, "the sight of my wife's life in jeopardy . . . terrifies me, and it is unbearable to see her suffering so much."[38] Camille finally died at the age of thirty-two in September 1879. Monet was left to care for their two sons, one twelve years old, the other an infant. In a last gesture to the woman he had painted so many times over their fourteen-year relationship, Monet immortalized the fading colors of his wife's face in *Camille on Her Deathbed*.

Monet's wife, Camille, died in 1879. He immortalized her one last time in *Camille on Her Deathbed*.

Winter Works

In the winter following Camille's death, France had record-setting cold temperatures that froze the Seine. During this unprecedented weather, Monet braved sub-zero temperatures to record the freeze and the subsequent thaw on canvas. In paintings such as *Ice Floes on the Seine*, *The Frost*, and *Sunset at*

Lavancourt, Monet rendered scenes of desolate beauty, with bare trees, cold winter light, and massive ice blocks floating down the river. However, as Potts points out:

> Although the subject matter itself could represent Monet's personal desolation, his treatment of it suggests that this is not the case. *The Frost* shows ice and frost sparkling in the sunlight, the white frost warmed up with pink and blue. Although a barren scene, the colors used give it a warmth. . . . The whole scene is harmonized through the use of strong horizontal [brush] strokes on the ice and small vertical strokes on the bushes. The vertical of the poplars balances the horizontal of the river bank.[39]

Whatever Monet's mental state in the winter of 1879, he was not alone with his children. His family shared the large house at Vétheuil with Ernest Hoschedé, Hoschedé's wife,

Monet painted *The Frost* during a record-setting cold winter in France.

Alice, their five daughters, and their infant son. Monet had invited the couple to live with him after Ernest lost his vast wealth, his estate, and his art collection during bankruptcy proceedings in 1877. With the two families living together and only Monet's income to support them, little money was left to pay the gardener, maid, and cook, all of whom sued Monet for failure to pay wages. Matters were further complicated when it became apparent that Monet and Alice were involved in a romantic relationship that had been going on for several years. When Ernest discovered this, he moved out of the Vétheuil house.

Hoping to improve his financial situation, Monet entered *Ice Floes on the Seine* and *Sunset at Lavancourt* in the 1880 Salon. *Lavancourt* was accepted, but "skyed," or placed so high on the uppermost row of paintings that it could not be easily viewed. Disgusted once again with the Paris art establishment, Monet began to pursue new methods for selling his paintings. His first attempt, a one-artist exhibition held in June 1880, yielded immediate results, and he sold several of his recent canvases. Later, Monet entered his paintings in provincial exhibitions in towns such as Grenoble and Nancy. Although he considered these small art shows beneath his status as a master painter, he was able to meet new collectors through this venture.

Painting the Normandy Coast

Monet's efforts brought him twelve thousand francs in 1880, but he still did not have enough money to cover his expenses. After conversations about the problem with Durand-Ruel, Monet became convinced that he could make money painting seascapes, which appealed to collectors more than his recent works. The artist had always loved the beauty of the Normandy coast along the English Channel. In early 1881 he made the first of many trips to the region to paint stark renderings of the plunging cliffs, desolate beaches, and crashing seas near the villages of Fécamp, Pourville, Varengeville, and Étretat. Over the next five years Monet traveled extensively to the Normandy coast, filling hundreds of canvases with the magnificent scenery found in the region.

"THE LIFE OF A LANDSCAPIST"

In 1886 French poet and novelist Guy de Maupassant accompanied Monet as he painted the Normandy Coast. During this period, the artist was painting a series of canvases of a single subject. Maupassant wrote the following in an article, "The Life of a Landscapist," for the magazine Le Gil-Blas:

Last year . . . I often followed Claude Monet, who was in search of impressions. Actually he was no longer a painter but a hunter [of spontaneous images]. He went along followed by children who carried his canvases, five or six canvases all depicting the same subject at different hours of the day and with different effects. He would take [the canvases] up in turn, then put them down again, depending on the changes in the sky. Standing before his subjects, he waited, watched the sun and the shadows, capturing in a few brushstrokes a falling ray of light or a passing cloud and, scorning false and conventional [painting] techniques, transferred them rapidly onto his canvas. In this way I saw him catch a sparkling stream of light on a white cliff and fix it in a flow of yellow tones that strangely rendered the surprising . . . effect of that elusive and blinding brilliance. Another time he caught with both hands a torrent of rain on the sea and flung it on his canvas [in a shower of paint]. It was truly rain that he had thus painted, nothing but rain throwing a veil over the waves, rocks, and sky, which could scarcely be discerned under this deluge.

Guy de Maupassant, "The Life of a Landscapist," *Le Gil-Blas*, September 28, 1886. Quoted in Charles F. Stuckey, ed., *Monet: A Retrospective*. New York: Park Lane, pp. 122–23.

Guy de Maupassant wrote about Monet when he accompanied him to the Normandy coast.

Compared with his views of the Seine completed in Argenteuil and Vétheuil, the Normandy paintings are much more dramatic. The reflection of the light in the ocean, the shades of the foliage on the cliffs, and the grandeur of the clouds at sunset are all brought alive by Monet's extensive mix, or juxtaposition, of warm colors next to cold colors. These techniques are exemplified in *The Cliffs at Grainval Near Fécamp*, where dozens of shades of aquamarine green in the sea fade into blue and purple near the shore, contrasting with shades of green, orange, pink, and burgundy along the cliff top. Each brushstroke seems to be of a different color. Single strokes are weaved into an intricate pattern, like individual threads on a brightly colored piece of cloth.

The *Cliffs at Grainval Near Fécamp* was one of a series of Grainval paintings created from the same vantage point. In reflecting his philosophy that "landscape is nothing but an impression—an instantaneous one,"[40] Monet sat and waited for hours watching the sun, waves, and shadows shift. When the moment struck, the artist recorded his impression of the spectacular view in a series of quick brushstrokes. Later, when the light and weather changed, he returned to a small stone house built high above the cliffs to record another scene. The angle from which the artist painted the cliffs from his perch is called a "seagull's view" by Robert L. Herbert in *Monet on the Normandy Coast*, who writes that "it is an aerial suspension that Monet will exploit repeatedly in coming years."[41]

Monet's Normandy paintings were well received at the Seventh Exhibition of Independent Artists, and the reviews were overwhelmingly positive as this 1883 review by Gustave Geffroy in *La Justice* demonstrates:

[The] painter exhausts himself to render the nuances of the color, all the accidents of the light. With the juxtaposition of pure colors, he succeeds in expressing planes . . . distance, and movement. He successfully analyzes the constantly changing and moving color of the flowing water, which crashes and foams at the foot of boulders and cliffs. He shows how [his choice of] color is determined by the state of the watery depths, the condition of the sky, and of the reflection of objects. He studies the land, the sunken dunes, and the sides of cliffs like a geologist. With the lip of his brush, he illuminates all the stones, all the minerals, and all the veins within the rocks. He considers all external influences. He paints the grass that has been dried by the wind and drenched by the rain. He skillfully reproduces the wet rocks, uncovered by the low tide, upon which the sea has left clumps of weeds.[42]

Interest from Art Collectors

The good reviews led to increased interest from art collectors, prompting Monet to return to the Normandy coast in February 1882 for seven weeks. The paintings created on this trip were promptly purchased by Durand-Ruel, inspiring Monet to return to the English Channel in the summer. This time he took along Alice and the couple's seven children. Paintings such as *Gorge of the Petit Ailly, Cliffs at Varengeville*, and *Cliff Walks at Pourville* were among the nearly ninety pictures the artist painted that summer.

Another trip in October yielded more canvases, and all were purchased by his art dealer, bringing his yearly income for 1882 to thirty-one thousand francs, more than two and a half times what he had made in previous years. Clearly, a good market existed for Monet's Impressionist renderings of Normandy. However, as Herbert writes:

> This does not mean Monet thought he was well off . . . for he continued to spend more than he earned, and at every stage owed his dealer yet more paintings against advances. He also had a backlog of unpaid bills and was threatened with [legal proceedings] in July for nonpayment of a debt of 1,200 francs going back fifteen years; he expected Durand-Ruel to provide the money.[43]

Driven by financial need, Monet continued with his travels in search of inspirational scenery. In early 1883 the artist went to Étretat. Here he created twenty-five canvases in three weeks, painting from the window of his hotel when the weather was too cold to work outdoors. The Étretat region proved to be one of the artist's favorites, and in the following three years Monet produced about seventy-five more paintings there, fifty of them in the cold light of winter or fall.

Spectacular Étretat Scenery

The Étretat paintings differ from the earlier seascapes because of the incredible scenery found in the region. Over the centuries the coast along this part of the Channel was carved by wind and water into three dramatic arches that curve out from the cliffs and plunge into the sea. The most spectacular arch,

Monet's Étretat paintings are known for the incredible scenery in the area. Monet painted the Manneporte arch several times in these pieces of artwork.

PAINTING IN A HURRICANE

Monet seemed to thrive on inclement weather and often painted in desolate regions while tempests raged around him. In Monet, Jean-Jacques Leveque quotes an anonymous source who watched Monet paint several canvases at the same time on the Normandy Coast:

[*A* witness reported having seen] Claude Monet wrapped in a cloak, the rain streaming over him, as he painted in the hurricane, doused by great splashes of salt water. He held two or three canvases between his knees, which at intervals of a few minutes he rotated on the easel. They all framed the same section of a cliff with the raging sea, under different lighting effects, fine infiltrations of light falling through breaks in the clouds. . . . The painter stalked each of these effects, a slave to the coming and going of light, halting his brush at the close of each of its appearances, setting at his feet the incomplete canvas . . . to resume . . . another work.

Jean-Jacques Leveque, *Monet*. New York: Crescent, 1990, p. 88.

Manneporte, which Monet painted several times, is located next to a pyramid of rock, called the Needle, which juts up out of the water. Tucker describes the Manneporte arch: "By its isolation and sheer size, it was both frightening and awe-inspiring, incomprehensible and yet incredibly physical."[44] Above the arches, bright green, lush grass provides a contrast to the sand-colored rock and blue seas below.

Danger as well as beauty lurked beneath the Manneporte arch. To visit the cove below, hikers had to time their walk to coincide with the low tide. When the tide rose the crashing waves made access to the cove impossible. Over the years some visitors had been trapped below the arch and swept into the ocean to drown. In November 1885 this almost happened to Monet, who, while concentrating on a painting, was thrown against the cliffs by a large wave. The artist, along with his canvas, easel, and paints, was then pulled into the ocean. After a narrow escape, he wrote to Alice, "My immediate thought was that I was done for, as the water dragged me down, but in the end I managed to clamber out on all fours."[45] The canvas, however, was torn to shreds by the waves and rocks, and Monet was angry that he could no longer work until he obtained more art supplies.

Monet put himself in danger because he was seeking new views of Manneporte that had never been put to canvas. This part of France had been painted extensively by Gustave Courbet in the 1870s as well as by dozens of other landscape artists of the early 1800s. This forced Monet to devise new ways of portraying the cliffs so his canvases would be unique. In pursuit of originality, the artist struggled to find new vantage points, painting the arches from the beach, from high above in his hotel room, and from close up. He also portrayed them during winter storms, calm seas, with beaches and boats, at sunset, and at high tide (from a safe distance). While painting outdoors in the most extreme conditions, Monet worked in high winds, anchoring his easel with ropes and rocks, wearing heavy winter clothes, or dressing like a fisherman in a hooded oilskin raincoat and rubber boots. However, the artist seemed to thrive in the turbulent weather, writing in the winter of 1886 to Durand-Ruel, "I don't know if the work I bring back will be to everyone's taste . . . but what I do know is that this coast enthralls me."[46]

Finding a House in Giverny

When Monet first began painting the Normandy coast in 1881, he was living in Vétheuil. In April 1883, however, the artist moved with his extended family to the farming village of Giverny, on the east bank of the Seine at the confluence of the Epte River. This scenic town of about three hundred farmers, 49 miles (80km) northwest of Paris, would be Monet's home until his death in 1926.

Monet rented the largest residence in the town, a pink stucco house on 2.5 acres (1ha). It was known as Le Pressoir or the Cider Press, for the apple cider made from the estate's orchard. As with his earlier moves, Monet chose Giverny for the artistic possibilities offered by the region, telling Durand-Ruel,

Monet moved to Giverny in 1883 and stayed there until his death in 1926.

"Once settled, I hope to produce masterpieces . . . because I like the countryside very much."[47]

Despite the declaration to his art dealer, Monet did not paint in the Giverny region for many years. Immediately after his family moved in, on April 30, 1883, Manet died at the age of fifty-one, and Monet traveled to Paris to attend the funeral. The artist then spent the summer painting on the Normandy coast. Then, at the end of the year Monet left northern France for the first time since 1870, traveling with Renoir to the Italian Riviera along the coast of the Mediterranean Sea. This was meant to be a painting trip, but Monet felt uncomfortable working with Renoir looking over his shoulder and did not paint on the trip. However, Monet appreciated the scenic value of the exquisite seaside palm trees, olive trees, and orange groves beneath the bright southern sun.

Overwhelming Beauty of the Mediterranean

In early 1884 Monet traveled alone to the Italian village of Bordighera on the Riviera. Describing the artistic possibilities of the region, Monet wrote to Alice:

> It's going to be rather painful for people who can't stand blue and pink, because it's precisely that brilliance, that enchanted light that I'm trying to catch, and anyone who hasn't visited this part of the world will . . . believe I've invented it, although actually I'm underplaying the tonal intensity: everything is the blue of a pigeon's neck or the color of flaming punch.[48]

This beauty, however, overwhelmed the artist, and at times he was fearful that he could not capture it on canvas, telling Durand-Ruel: "It is a magical and terribly difficult land. I would need a palette of diamonds and jewels"[49] to recreate the colors.

Despite his insecurities, Monet returned to Giverny with fifty canvases of Italy including *Bordighera* and *Villas at Bordighera*. The painting *Olive Grove in Moreno Gardens* was created in lavish gardens described by Monet as "pure fairly-and."[50] These gardens, owned by wealthy art patron Francesco Moreno, inspired Monet to plant his own sumptuous gardens at Giverny in later years.

Monet was rewarded financially from his work on the Mediterranean. His dealer bought twenty-one of the canvases. These were quickly purchased by collectors, bringing the artist's total income in 1884 to forty-five thousand francs, an enormous sum for someone who had lived so long in poverty.

In 1886 Monet became an internationally recognized artist when Durand-Ruel sent fifty of his canvases to New York City for the exhibition "Works in Oil and Pastel by the Impressionists

The beauty of the Bordighera region overwhelmed Monet and he was fearful that he could not capture what he saw on canvas. Despite his fears, he painted fifty canvases including Villas at Bordighera.

in Paris" at the American Art Gallery. The exhibition of three hundred paintings by French artists was extremely popular, and Monet's large contribution garnered widespread critical praise.

Battling the Elements on Belle-Isle

The money, prestige, and good reviews barely slowed Monet's prolific pace, and the artist remained passionately dedicated to painting. On a trip to Belle-Île, or Belle-Isle, an island in the Atlantic off the western coast of France, Monet painted forty canvases between September and December 1886. These paintings capture the violent beauty of the southwest side of the island known as the "Wild Coast," where assaults by the wind and the sea carved dangerously steep cliffs and towering arches in the hard, black basalt rock.

Monet hired a porter to help him cart his art supplies and ten canvases to the roughest, most inaccessible areas of the Wild Coast. However, after two days the overburdened porter quit, leaving Monet with seven canvases he had already started. To make matters worse, gusty winds, rain squalls, and thunderstorms battered the artist, carrying off his canvases or blowing his palette and brushes from his hand. Nonetheless, Monet was happiest when fighting the elements to capture his impressions of rugged scenery, telling Alice:

> I'm happier than I was, I've seen some wonderful sights and I'm going to . . . the area known as *la Mer Terrible* [the Terrible Sea] which is aptly named: there isn't a tree within miles, and the rocks and caves are fantastic; it's as sinister as hell, but quite superb . . . so different from the Channel coast that I'm having to familiarize myself with the scenery here; the sea is very beautiful, as for the rocks, they are an extraordinary combination of grottoes, outcrops and needles.[51]

When Monet did familiarize himself with scenery, he produced paintings unlike those created on the English Channel coast. Gone were images of misty seas and luminous clouds.

"The Light Is Simply Terrifying"

When Monet traveled to Bordighera on the Italian Riviera in 1884, he was overwhelmed by the tropical Mediterranean scenery. The color, light, and brilliant blue southern sky was completely different from northern France, where he had been painting for more than thirty years. In a letter home to Alice Hoschedé, Monet describes the difficulty he was having adapting his palette to this new range of light and color:

I am slaving away on six paintings a day. I'm giving myself a hard time over it as I haven't yet managed to capture the color of this landscape; there are moments when I'm appalled at the colors I'm having to use, I'm afraid what I'm doing is just dreadful and yet I really am understating it; the light is simply terrifying. I have already spent six sessions on some studies, but it's all so new to me that I can't quite bring them off; however the joy of it here is that each day I can return to the same [lighting] effect, so it's possible to track down and do battle with an effect. That's why I'm working so feverishly . . . I can be bold and include every tone of pink and blue: it's enchanting, it's delicious, and I hope it will please you.

Claude Monet, *Monet by Himself*, ed. Richard Kendall. Boston: Bulfinch, 1989, p. 109.

Instead, the sky is completely absent from the Belle-Isle works. The canvases are filled with stark rocks and turbulent bluish black waves frozen in the moment, or as Potts says, dashed off "in a frenzy of excitement."[52]

Capturing Moments of Light

The spontaneity of the Belle-Isle paintings can be traced to the new painting technique Monet developed during this time. The artist would set up three or four canvases next to one another. As the light changed or the tide shifted the waves, Monet would move from one canvas to the next, painting for no more than a few minutes, capturing an instant image, and moving down the line to the next painting. These canvases were finished where they were begun. Monet never touched up the paintings or changed them later in his studio.

Using this method, Monet created forty Belle-Isle canvases that reflect an intense study of a single locale. This led art critic Gustave Geffroy to write that Monet captured "the sea, where all is in continuous motion—the shape of the waves, the transparent depths, the variety of foam, the reflections of the sky."[53] Not everyone appreciated the results of Monet's new painting technique, however. Fellow Impressionist Pissarro said the Belle-Isle pictures did "not represent a highly developed art," while Degas said Monet was more interested in money than art, and the paintings were "made to sell."[54]

Monet's colleagues failed to appreciate that the artist was entering a new phase in his career. In this phase Monet would paint the same subject over and over, capturing the changing light of day and the shifting weather conditions. By doing so, Monet earned widespread praise and financial rewards. More important to Monet himself, he finally gained recognition as one of France's greatest painters. His place in history was established, and his paintings would be admired by millions for countless years to come.

At Home
in Giverny

In September 1888 Monet was out for a morning walk in the fields around Giverny with Suzanne Hoschedé, Alice's teenage daughter. It was harvest time and the local farmers had built giant haystacks in the fields, much as they had done every September for the past thousand years. These large round bundles of tied wheat stalks were 20 feet (6m) high and protected from the elements by cone-shaped thatched roofs which sat atop the grain. This method of storing wheat was so common in the French countryside that few passersby took notice of the haystacks in the fields.

Monet, however, saw the natural beauty of the colors, shadows, and arrangements of the stacks. He sent Suzanne to bring two canvases, his easel, and paints from his studio so he could capture the haystacks immediately in direct sunlight and later when the clouds covered the sun. However, as Monet recalls the story, by the time Suzanne returned, "I noticed that the light had changed. I said to [her], 'Would you go back to the house, please, and bring me another canvas?' She brought it to me, but very soon the light had changed again. 'One more!' and, 'One more still!'"[55] In this manner, Monet painted the first five paintings in his famous *Haystacks* series, also called *Wheatstacks* or *Grainstacks*. The series eventually included thirty paintings.

The following spring, with the idea of making series paintings foremost in his mind, Monet took a trip to the Creuse Valley in central France, where he painted fourteen canvases. Seven of the paintings depicted a single subject, the Creuse Canyon, formed by the confluence of the Grande and Petit Creuse rivers. Every painting in the series was of uniform size, and each was created during a limited period of time. But the individual paintings are different due to the atmospheric effects of the sunlight, the clouds, the weather, and the time of day. Universally praised by critics when they were exhibited in the summer of 1889, Monet entered a new phase of his career.

For the next thirty years, with a few exceptions, the artist would limit his subject matter to five motifs: stacks of wheat, poplars, the Rouen Cathedral in northwestern France, structures along the Thames River in London, and his garden pond in Giverny. Few artists could have achieved success with such self-imposed limitations. But Monet's mastery of color, subtle details, brushwork, and composition meant that each individual canvas evoked different moods and emotions depending on the spontaneous moment when it was created. Painted by the master Impressionist, each canvas was unique.

Wheatstacks in the Envelope

In the fall of 1890 Monet became so obsessed with painting haystacks he was late delivering several paintings of oat fields and poppies he had sold to Durand-Ruel. The paintings he had promised to his art dealer were important. Monet had already spent the advance money as a down payment on the Cider Press estate, purchased on November 17 for twenty-two thousand francs, just three days after his fiftieth birthday.

The delivery had to wait because the fall was exceptionally warm, and Monet wanted to take full advantage of the weather to work in the open air. Even when snow began to fall, the temperatures were mild enough for the artist to work in the open air. During this period he created *Wheatstacks (Full Sunlight)*, *Wheatstacks (Sunset)*, and *Wheatstacks (Effects of Snow, Morning)*. How-

During this period, Monet became obsessed with painting haystacks and created twenty-five in this series. Pictured here is *Haystacks in the Sun, Morning Effect*.

Monet painted at different times of day to create his haystack paintings, including *Haystacks at Sunset*.

ever, Monet was so consumed with capturing the haystacks on canvas that he took no pleasure from his work, telling Geffroy:

> I'm hard at it, working stubbornly on a series of different effects (grain stacks), but at this time of year the sun sets so fast that it's impossible to keep up with it. . . . I'm getting so slow at my work it makes me despair, but the further I get, the more I see a lot of work has

to be done in order to render what I'm looking for: "Instantaneity," the "envelope" above all, the same light spread over everything.[56]

Monet often referred to the envelope in correspondences. While difficult for some to understand, the envelope was Monet's term for seeing the momentary blend of light, atmospheric haze, and other weather conditions as a single unit. This entity enveloped, or covered, a subject for an instant. This might mean that a fine mist in the air blocked out the view of distant objects or a crisp winter air allowed the sun to shine brightly on a haystack. Throughout the 1890s Monet was passionate in his pursuit of the envelope. He felt this aspect of painting had been ignored by other artists who were more concerned with accurate depictions of people and things.

Whether or not art collectors understood Monet's envelope, they were astounded by his haystacks. In April 1891 the demand for the fifteen canvases Monet had painted over the winter was remarkable, with offers of five thousand to six thousand francs for each painting. Before selling them, however, Monet had a one-artist exhibition at the Durand-Ruel Gallery, in which all of the *Wheatstacks* were hung side by side. Monet explained the purpose of the exhibition to a visitor, saying "the full value of [one painting] is not apparent except by comparison [with the others] in the succession of the series as a whole."[57]

Poplars Along the Epte River

Monet eventually painted a total of twenty-five haystack paintings, but even before his Paris exhibition of the *Wheatstacks* began he was at work on his next series: the poplars along the Epte River, about 1.2 miles (2km) from his house. Monet painted these tall vertical trees as he observed them in different climatic conditions and seasons. As with the haystacks, the artist painted the same subjects repeatedly, sometimes waiting for hours or days for the exact moment that he wished to capture on canvas.

In style and color, however, the new paintings were quite different from the *Haystacks* series. While Monet painted

the haystacks from a distance, he observed the poplars from his studio boat low in the water, painting the slender tree trunks jutting up to fill the tops of the canvases with shimmering color. In addition, the shadows and light reflected off the river are rendered in heightened contrast, with sharp

Poplars on the Epte River astonished Paris critics because of its freshness and unique effects.

THE POETRY OF POPLARS

The graceful composition and colors of Monet's Poplar *series inspired art critic Clément Janin to describe the canvases in poetic terms in an 1892 exhibition review published in* L'Estafette:

What is it? Not much. Three or four poplars on the edge of a marsh. Their trunks are reflected in the water, the hair of their heads quivers in the sky; farther away, other poplars recede along the road. This is repeated fifteen times, at all hours of the day, with all the variations in appearance brought to things by changes in the surrounding atmosphere and light; here, the clear sweet song of the end of a summer day, before night falls but when already the sky is becoming like watered silk and [an anxious shimmer] of light amethyst and turquoise disturbs the cerulean [blue] serenity of the horizon; there, in the fierce depths of the infinite, gather the dark shades of lapis lazuli through which the rays of sun are concentrated and burn; elsewhere, like pink sailing boats on Oriental seas, fragile clouds driven by the evening breeze, flow pink against a sky of forget-me-nots, and everywhere the poplars sleep, breathe, and murmur, lifting up their supple trunks, mingling their [unfolding beauty], living their own lives within that great collective life of nature.

Quoted in Robert Gordon and Andrew Forge, *Monet*. New York: Harry N. Abrams, 1985, p. 167.

divisions between the blues and yellows, the purples and oranges. Regarding the composition, the squat shape of the haystacks gives way to a graceful S-curve of trees. Sweeping arches of foliage move down the canvases from the foreground to the distance.

Like Monet's previous series, the names of individual paintings were simply functional: *Poplars Along the Epte River*

(Autumn), Poplars Along the Epte River (Sunset Effect), and *Poplars Along the Epte River (Dusk).* And once again the paintings astonished the Paris art world with their freshness and unique effects. When they were exhibited at the Durand-Ruel Gallery in March 1892, one of Monet's close friends, novelist and playwright Octave Mirbeau, succinctly expressed the public's attitude in a letter to the artist:

> It is an absolutely magnificent work . . . I felt complete joy, an emotion that I can't express. . . . The beauty of those lines, the newness of those lines and their grandeur, and the immensity of the sky and the thrill of it all . . . you hear me, my dear Monet, never, never has an artist expressed such things, and it is again a revelation of a new Monet. . . . I am overwhelmed.[58]

Collectors were also overwhelmed, and many of the fifteen canvases were sold even before the exhibition began. Others sold in a matter of days.

Transitions of Light at the Rouen Cathedral

By the time the *Poplar* series was attracting such positive attention, Monet was living in a room above a shop on the Rue Grand-Pont in Rouen. He had rented the room to observe the facade of the ancient Rouen Cathedral, marked by spiraling towers and lacy Gothic stonework. Original construction on the cathedral was begun in the thirteenth century, and it was added to over the years. For Monet, painting a series of pictures of a building was a departure from the nature canvases he had been creating for more than ten years. And this series, unlike the poplars, was not completed in a matter of months. The artist worked on the canvases in early 1892 before taking a break for about one year. During the time away from his canvases, Monet married his longtime girlfriend Alice Hoschedé on July 16, 1892.

Monet resumed painting the Rouen Cathedral in the spring of 1893, and he worked on the paintings in his home studio for another year. The artist had never worked on a single motif for such an extended period, especially an architectural subject. The result of his efforts was a series of twenty canvases including *Rouen Cathedral, Façade (Gray Day)*, *Rouen Cathedral, Façade (Morning Effect)*, and *Rouen Cathedral, the Façade in Sunlight*.

Journalist Georges Clemenceau divided the Rouen paintings into four general categories: the gray series, the white series, the rainbow series, and the blue series. Writing in *La*

Monet painted the Rouen Cathedral twenty different times during the course of a year, capturing impressions and colors as the weather and seasons changed.

Claude Monet stands in his gardens at his estate in Giverny, France.

Justice, Clemenceau explained: "Imagine them aligned . . . according to transitions of light: the great black mass in the beginning of the gray series, constantly growing lighter, to the white series, going from the molten light to bursting [colors] that continue and are achieved in the fires of the rainbow series, which subside in the calm of the blue series and fade away in the divine mist of azure."[59]

Monet did not exhibit the *Rouen Cathedral* series until May 1895, his first show in three years. By this time anticipation was high, and the exhibition caused a great sensation marked by both high praise and unkind criticism. Several reviewers complained that Monet's colors were unrealistic and the lack of details made the canvases seem unfinished. However, congratulations came from an unlikely source, Monet's fellow Impressionists who had been harshly critical of the poplar and haystack canvases. Pissarro said he was "carried away by their extraordinary deftness [and] Cézanne is in complete agreement."[60]

Monet recognized his own achievement and was asking fifteen thousand francs for each cathedral canvas, three times more than the poplars and five times more than the haystacks.

Monet used his gardens at Giverny as an artistic muse. In Monet: Late Paint-ings of Giverny from the Musée Marmottan, author, gardener, and photog-rapher Elizabeth Murray describes the beauty of Monet's water lily pond:

Monet created his water-lily garden for beauty. What he found was endless inspiration and tranquility. His greatest passion and challenge was to paint the fleeting quality of light. In his water garden he discovered infinite motifs. The pond was a mirror reflecting each nuance of atmospheric change—a moving cloud, a ripple of wind, a coming storm. It held inverted images of the surrounding landscape [reflected in the water] while simultaneously supporting thousands of floating water flowers. The effect was that of a prism in the light, spreading shimmering shades of precious gold, ruby, amethyst, sapphire, and topaz over the surface of the water. These flowers were like multifaceted jewels on deep green settings of round, floating, palette-shaped leaves. The pond thus became the focal point for Monet, which he treated with reverence, as a personal sanctuary.

Lynn Federle Orr, Paul Hayes Tucker, and Elizabeth Murray, *Monet: Late Paintings of Giverny from the Musée Marmottan*. New Orleans: New Orleans Museum of Art, 1994, p. 55.

Monet's gardens and pond inspired many of his most beloved paintings.

While his art dealer initially advised against asking such high prices, the cathedral paintings sold quickly.

Planting a Garden

After this string of successes, Monet took time away from his canvases to develop his estate at Giverny. With his expert painter's eye for color, light, and composition, he began transforming the grounds into magnificent gardens, spending long hours paging through seed catalogs and discussing plant specimens with French gardening experts. Monet laid out several acres of raised planters, fertilized flower beds, and trellises that arched over sand paths. A wide variety of flowers from across the globe was planted, and they were coordinated to bloom continuously from early spring until late autumn.

Monet also upgraded a small marshy pond on his property, enlarging it to four times its original size by diverting a small stream from the Epte River. According to his statement on the building permit, the purpose of the expansion was to create a spectacular water garden "for the pleasure of the eye and also for motifs to paint,"[61] Other improvements included the construction of a decorative Japanese-style wooden bridge where the stream flowed into the pond. This was surrounded by wisterias, weeping willows, Japanese apple trees, and bamboo. The pond was filled with nympheas, or water lilies, that bloomed all summer. Monet employed a team of gardeners to pick weeds from the bottom of the pond and scoop up algae so that the water retained a mirrorlike reflective surface. Monet could afford these projects since his income was now more than 100,000 francs a year. However, as he told one interviewer, "Everything I have earned has gone into these gardens."[62]

A Dazzling Display of Light

Monet did not make many paintings of his gardens, since they did not reach maturity for many years. But after painting the splendor of nature for so many years, Monet decided to create another architectural series, checking into the luxurious Savoy Hotel in London in September 1899. Monet's room was on

Monet created another architectural series by painting the Houses of Parliament in London.

The Houses of Parliament, Sunset (top) and Parliament, Sunlight Effects in the Fog (bottom) are considered some of the most remarkable of Monet's London series.

the sixth floor and offered a stunning view of the Thames River and south London. Using this room as his base, Monet made three extended painting trips to London during the following three years, creating over one hundred canvases of three subjects, the Charing Cross Bridge and the Waterloo Bridge across the Thames, and the Houses of Parliament, where the legislature for the United Kingdom conducts business. Monet explained why he took up this unprecedented project: "What I like most of all in London is the fog. . . . Without the fog, London would not be a beautiful city. It's the fog that gives it its magnificent breadth."[63]

London's fog at that time was actually smog, a mixture of fog and air pollution caused by the widespread use of coal. Nevertheless, the thick blanket of fog, the weak sun, and the smothered light created unusual atmospheric conditions found nowhere else in the world. To Monet this environment provided a beautiful envelope that he layered over the ancient buildings, the industrialism of the trains and traffic on the bridges, the factories in the distance, and the boats on the water. Of all the paintings made in London, those such as *The Houses of Parliament, Sunset* and *Parliament, Sunlight Effects in the Fog* are considered the most remarkable, as Tucker explains:

[The dramatic weather effects] abound in the views of the Houses of Parliament where the often obscured orb of the sun pushes out from behind the almost impenetrable cloak of clouds and the haunting silhouettes of the Gothic-revival buildings to shoot its rays of orange, yellow, and red across the darkened sky and river. Unidentified except by outline, the Houses of Parliament in these pictures appear like specters, their towers rising to various heights. . . . As in his *Cathedral* paintings, the buildings also seem to celebrate the magical, transformative powers of light. They stretch upwards to greet it and then stand like solemn sentinels as it spreads across the sky. Occasionally, Monet makes these associations more theatrical . . . where the quivering towers seem to have set off an explosion of electrical energy, creating a dazzling display of light in the heavens.[64]

When Monet finally exhibited the massive collection of the *London* series masterpieces in 1904, the show was met with universal acclaim. Art historian Gustave Kahn labeled Monet a "master composer of [artistic] symphonies."[65] English artist Wynford Dewhurst noted Monet "is one of the few original members of the Impressionist group who has lived to see the . . . complete reversal of the hostile judgment passed upon his canvases by an ill-educated public."[66] Delighted at his triumph, Monet, now sixty-three-years old, returned to his beloved Giverny gardens, which were now so lush and beautiful that they would provide him with artistic inspiration for the rest of his life.

The Japanese Bridge and Water Lilies

In between painting trips to London, Monet focused his artistic eye on subjects closer to home, especially the water lilies growing in his pond in Giverny. In 1899 the artist painted eighteen canvases of his Japanese bridge arching over hundreds of violet-colored water lilies and framed by a weeping willow and other trees. Some of the paintings are rendered in muted colors that reflect an overcast rainy afternoon. Other paintings, such as *The Water Lily Pond (Japanese Bridge)*, are almost garish for their liberal use of sunbathed colors such as canary yellow, lime green, purple-pink, orange, and fiery red, capturing what critic Charles Saunier calls "a suffocating heat [that] creates rainbow-like effects."[67]

The Japanese bridge paintings were undoubtedly influenced by Monet's love of Japanese art prints and by the painting *Wisteria* by Utagawa Hiroshige. However, in the work that followed, Monet dispensed with the bridge completely, painting only the water lilies and reflections in the pond, creating eighty such canvases between 1903 and 1908. This was a much more difficult task, as the bridge gave a conventional sense of perspective and depth to the paintings. Successfully capturing the infinitely changing surface of the shimmering water, the irregular shapes of the water lilies, and mirror images of clouds above proved to be difficult even for a master such as Monet. The artist's feelings were revealed in an 1908 letter to Geffroy: "These landscapes of water and reflection have become an obsession. It's quite beyond my powers at my age, and yet I want to succeed in expressing what I feel."[68]

Monet exhibited the first of the water lily paintings that same year, and the paintings sold for record amounts. The artist was now a millionaire who used his money to purchase

Monet painted eighteen canvases of his Japanese bridge, including *The Japanese Footbridge and the Water Lily Pool,* capturing it in different stages and light.

The *Water Lily* series comprises numerous paintings, and today they are shown in galleries all over the world.

fine suits, expensive food, and some of the first automobiles in France. He also traveled throughout Europe and built a greenhouse on his property along with a second studio and a darkroom where he pursued his growing interest in photography.

More Personal Tragedy

Money and fame could not prevent harsh reality from intruding on Monet's well-constructed life. In the spring of 1910 the Seine and Epte rivers overflowed, swamping his beloved gardens and nearly flooding his home. During this period, Alice was diagnosed with leukemia and suffered in great pain until her death in May 1911. After his wife's death, the seventy-year-old Monet was lost in grief for months and refused to paint. However, at the end of the year he picked up his brushes once again, finishing twenty-nine canvases he had begun in Venice, Italy, on one of the last vacations he took with Alice.

Monet's work was interrupted once more in 1912 when he suddenly realized he could not see clearly out of his right eye. Doctors told Monet he had developed nuclear cataracts in both eyes. Cataracts create a milky film over the lens of the eye and eventually cause glaucoma which leads to blindness. Doctors recommended surgery on his right eye, but the cataract problem seemed to stabilize and he refused the operation.

Although cataracts distort the color perception and make it difficult to focus clearly, Monet was spurred to complete new projects before his eyesight failed completely. In 1915 he built a huge new studio, 75 feet (23m) by 40 feet (12m), with a glass-paneled roof that rose to a height of nearly 50 feet (15m). After completing this cavernous work space Monet lined the walls with nineteen huge canvas panels 6.5 feet (2m) high by 14 feet (4.25m) wide. The canvases were mounted on easels with wheels that could be moved around the studio and arranged in different combinations.

The *Grandes Décorations*

During the next several years Monet worked on a series of forty massive paintings he called *Grandes Décorations* or *Large Decorations*. These massive works focused on the light and atmosphere reflected in his lily pond. Four of the panels, simply called *Morning*, show lilies opening in the glittering light, displaying bright flowers over muted planes of water and floating leaves. *Green Reflections* shows the pond in the cool, refreshing shade of late afternoon, and *Sunset* renders the pond in the failing light.

The *Grandes Décorations* paintings, with their built-up crusts of multicolored paint layered onto canvases of immense scale with large brushes, were unlike anything Monet had ever attempted. Thick, pitted areas of pigment contrasted with thin, delicate sections of color, with dark shadows set against intense

MONET'S CATARACTS AND COLORS

Monet was first diagnosed with nuclear cataracts in both eyes in 1912, at the age of seventy-two. However, his visual problems began seven years earlier when he began to experience changes in his color perception. The Web article "Art, Vision & the Disordered Eye" explains how cataracts caused Monet to see distorted colors which were then committed to canvas by the artist:

[In] 1905, at age 65, he began to experience changes in his perception of color. He no longer perceived colors with the same intensity. Indeed his paintings showed a change in the whites and greens and blues, with a shift towards "muddier" yellow and purple tones. After 1915, his paintings became much more abstract, with an even more pronounced color shift from blue-green to red-yellow. He complained of perceiving reds as muddy, dull pinks, and other objects as yellow. These changes are consistent with the visual effects of cataracts. Nuclear cataracts absorb light, desaturate colors, and make the world appear more yellow.

Monet was both troubled and intrigued by the effects of his declining vision, as he reacted to the foggy, impressionistic personal world that he was famous for painting. In a [1922] letter to his friend J. Bernheim-Jeune he wrote, "To think I was getting on so well, more absorbed than I've ever been and expecting to achieve something, but… my poor eyesight makes me see everything in a complete fog. It's very beautiful all the same and it's this which I'd love to have been able to convey. All in all, I am very unhappy."

University of Calgary, "Art, Vision & the Disordered Eye," 2007. www.psych.ucalgary.ca/PACE/VA-Lab/AVDE-Website/monet.html.

highlights. In the pursuit of perfection, Monet relentlessly re-arranged the order of the canvases. When new paintings were placed together, he scraped off pigment and repainted and revised the pictures so they would merge with one another. By creating a series in this manner, Monet drew upon his more than seven decades of experience to create timeless, and priceless, works of splendor. When news of his unprecedented works and his huge new studio was described in the press, the road to Giverny was filled with artists and admirers making the pilgrimage from Paris to meet the great painter.

Monet Loses His Sight

In November 1923, with the *Grandes Décorations* nearly finished, Monet's eye doctor informed him he was blind in his right eye and had only 10 percent sight in his left. The following January Monet finally underwent surgery to remove the cataract in his right eye. Two more operations were required in July 1924, and the artist's eyesight was partially restored. By this time the Musée de l'Orangerie in Paris was set to honor Monet by hanging twenty-two of the panels from *Grandes Décorations* in two oval-shaped rooms. The panels in the first room would reflect the changing effects of light on the lily pond from morning until sunset. The murals in the second room would consist of a panoramic view of the pond as seen through the drooping foliage of weeping willows.

Monet's *Water Lilies* exhibit was set to open on May 16, 1927, but during the winter of 1926 the artist became gravely ill, suffering from a lung tumor which led to a condition called pulmonary sclerosis. On December 5 Monet died around 1 P.M. His last gesture was to hold up two fingers a few inches apart to indicate to Clemenceau the width of the frames he wanted around his murals at the Musée de l'Orangerie. Three days later he was buried without religious ceremony beside Alice in the family plot in Giverny.

Monet's Legacy

During the first half of his career Monet often struggled to sell his paintings for a few hundred dollars to pay rent and buy

Pictured here is Room 1 of Monet's *Water Lilies* exhibit at the Musée de l'Orangerie in Paris.

food for his children. However, the artist lived long enough to sell his paintings for tens of thousands of dollars. By the time of his death he was honored as one of history's most talented and innovative artists. But even Monet would be shocked at the prices paid for his canvases in modern times. In June 2007 one of the artist's turn-of-the-century water lily paintings, *Nympheas*, sold for $36.5 million. At the same auction the 1904 canvas *Waterloo Bridge, Overcast Weather* sold for $35.5 million, nearly triple the presale estimated price. The artist's other works climb in value every year.

While Monet would undoubtedly be pleased at the recognition he now receives for pioneering the Impressionist school

of painting, in his lifetime he was rarely happy. Details from thousands of letters written by the artist show a man suffering almost daily while trying to commit his unique vision to canvas. He also suffered personal tragedies and was shown little respect for his talents until later in life. Through it all Monet created thousands of canvases and left a legacy not only of his personal talents but of a new way for painters to portray the world. Today, Monet's most famous works decorate posters, calendars, T-shirts, and even coffee mugs throughout the world. These Impressionist images have provided inspiration to generations past and will undoubtedly continue to do so for generations to come.

Notes

Introduction: Master of Impressionism

1. Quoted in Charles F. Stuckey, *Claude Monet: 1840–1926*. New York: Thames and Hudson, 1995, p. 8.
2. Stuckey, *Claude Monet: 1840–1926*, p. 9.

Chapter 1: The Early Years

3. Quoted in William C. Seitz, *Claude Monet*. New York: Harry N. Abrams, 1982, p. 10.
4. Quoted in Seitz, *Claude Monet*, p. 11.
5. Quoted in Sue Rose, *The Private Lives of the Impressionists*. New York: HarperCollins, 2006, p. 11.
6. Quoted in Seitz, *Claude Monet*, p. 13.
7. Quoted in Paul Hayes Tucker, *Claude Monet: Life and Art*. New Haven, CT: Yale University Press, 1995, p. 8.
8. Tucker, *Claude Monet: Life and Art*, p. 8.
9. Tucker, *Claude Monet: Life and Art*, p. 13.
10. Quoted in Tucker, *Claude Monet: Life and Art*, p. 13.

11. Tucker, *Claude Monet: Life and Art*, p. 14.
12. Rose, *The Private Lives of the Impressionists*, p. 12.
13. Jim Lane, "The Salon des Refusés," Humanities Web, September 20, 1998. www.humanitiesweb.org/human.php?s=g&p=a&a=i&ID=293.
14. Seitz, *Claude Monet*, p. 17.

Chapter 2: The Struggling Artist Breaks Through

15. Rose, *The Private Lives of the Impressionists*, pp. 44–45.
16. Vanessa Potts, *Monet*. Bath, England: Parragon, 2001, p. 28.
17. Quoted in Tucker, *Claude Monet: Life and Art*, p. 32.
18. Claude Monet, *Monet by Himself*, ed. Richard Kendall. Boston: Bulfinch, 1989, p. 25.
19. Jean-Paul Crespelle, *Monet*. London: Studio Editions, 1993, p. 13.
20. Monet, *Monet by Himself*, p. 26.
21. Monet, *Monet by Himself*, p. 26.
22. Sophie Monneret, *Monet: His Life and Complete Works*. Barcelona, Spain: Longview, 1995, p. 36.
23. Monet, *Monet by Himself*, p. 27.
24. Quoted in Crespelle, *Monet*, p. 14.

25. Monneret, *Monet: His Life and Complete Works*, pp. 38–39.

26. Tucker, *Claude Monet: Life and Art*, pp. 45–46.

Chapter 3: The Impression of Success at Argenteuil

27. Tucker, *Claude Monet: Life and Art*, p. 48.

28. John Piper, *British Romantic Artists*. London: Collins, 1946, p. 17.

29. Quoted in Tucker, *Claude Monet: Life and Art*, p. 49.

30. Paul Hayes Tucker, *The Impressionists at Argenteuil*. Washington, DC: National Gallery of Art, 2000, p. 21.

31. Tucker, *Claude Monet: Life and Art*, p. 55.

32. Don Morrison, "Monet's Love Affair with Japanese Art," Time.com, January 4, 2007. www.time.com/time/magazine/article/0,9171,1573943-2,00.html.

33. Quoted in Charles F. Stuckey, ed., *Monet: A Retrospective*. New York: Park Lane, pp. 58–59.

34. Quoted in Tucker, *Claude Monet: Life and Art*, p. 77.

35. Quoted in Stuckey, *Monet: A Retrospective*, p. 57.

36. Monneret, *Monet: His Life and Complete Works*, pp. 56–57.

Chapter 4: Painting His Way into History

37. Monet, *Monet by Himself*, p. 29.

38. Monet, *Monet by Himself*, p. 31.

39. Potts, *Monet*, p. 108.

40. Quoted in Katherine Tyrrell, "Making a Mark," Blogspot, February 19, 2006. http://makingamark.blogspot.com/2006/02/art-quotation-of-week-19-february-2006.html.

41. Robert L. Herbert, *Monet on the Normandy Coast*. New Haven, CT: Yale University Press, 1994, p. 39.

42. Quoted in Stuckey, *Monet: A Retrospective*, p. 96.

43. Herbert, *Monet on the Normandy Coast*, p. 43.

44. Tucker, *Claude Monet: Life and Art*, p. 115.

45. Monet, *Monet by Himself*, p. 115.

46. Quoted in Crespelle, *Monet*, p. 112.

47. Quoted in Metropolitan Museum of Art, *Monet's Years at Giverny: Beyond Impressionism*. New York: Harry N. Abrams, 1978, pp. 15–16.

48. Quoted in Crespelle, *Monet*, p. 31.

49. Quoted in *Claude Monet Life and Art*, "Painting Bordighera in the Riviera, Italy," September 30, 2006. www.intermonet.com/oeuvre/bordig.htm.

50. Quoted in Stuckey, *Monet: A Retrospective*, p. 210.

51. Monet, *Monet by Himself*, pp. 118–19.

52. Potts, *Monet*, p. 154.

53. Quoted in Stuckey, *Monet: A Retrospective*, p. 128.

54. Quoted in Tucker, *Claude Monet: Life and Art*, p. 133.

Chapter 5: At Home in Giverny

55. Quoted in Tucker, *Claude Monet: Life and Art*, p. 141.

56. Quoted in Monet and Kendall, *Monet by Himself*, p. 172.

57. Quoted in Stuckey, *Monet: A Retrospective*, p. 220.

58. Quoted in Robert Gordon and Andrew Forge, *Monet*. New York: Harry N. Abrams, 1985, p. 167.

59. Quoted in Stuckey, *Monet: A Retrospective*, pp. 179–80.

60. Quoted in Paul Hayes Tucker, *Monet in the '90s*. New Haven, CT: Yale University Press, 1989, p. 143.

61. Quoted in Tucker, *Monet in the '90s*, p. 255.

62. Quoted in Lynn Federle Orr, Paul Hayes Tucker, and Elizabeth Murray, *Monet: Late Paintings of Giverny from the Musée Marmottan*. New Orleans : New Orleans Museum of Art, 1994, p. 32.

63. Quoted in Tucker, *Monet in the '90s*, p. 244.

64. Tucker, *Claude Monet: Life and Art*, p. 168.

65. Quoted in Stuckey, *Monet: A Retrospective*, p. 226.

66. Quoted in Stuckey, *Monet: A Retrospective*, p. 232.

67. Quoted in Tucker, *Claude Monet: Life and Art*, p. 187.

68. Monet, *Monet by Himself*, p. 240.

Glossary

Barbizon School: A group of associated artists who made paintings of rural workers and the natural world around the rustic village of Barbizon, France.

bourgeois: An affluent middle-class person who is viewed as conservative, conventional, and materialistic.

bucolic: Describes a peaceful rural life.

caricature: A humorous cartoonlike drawing that depicts the subject with exaggerated physical features, such as a large nose or tiny legs.

en plein air: French for "in the open air," typically used to define paintings created outdoors.

estuary: A wide, marshy course of a river where its fresh current flows into the salty ocean tide.

stylized: Created in a distinctive style for artistic effect.

For Further Reading

Books

Richard Mühlberger, *What Makes a Monet a Monet?* New York: Metropolitan Museum of Art, 2002. Twelve of Monet's most important paintings are accompanied by analyses of composition, line, color, subject matter, and the world the artist lived and worked in.

Vanessa Potts, *Monet*. Bath, England: Parragon, 2001. Detailed commentary on 120 of Monet's works covering all aspects of his style, with full color reproductions of each painting.

Carol Sabbeth, *Monet and the Impressionists for Kids*. Chicago: Chicago Review, 2002. The author is an art teacher who provides an introduction to the nineteenth-century Impressionist movement, from the ill-received first exhibition to Monet's later acceptance. Also discussed are painters such as Renoir, Degas, Cézanne and Mary Cassatt.

Paul Hayes Tucker, *The Impressionists at Argenteuil*. Washington, DC: National Gallery of Art, 2000. This book, published for an ex-hibition at the National Gallery, presents the classic works produced around the French suburb of Argenteuil by Monet, Renoir, Manet, and others who have come to define Impressionism.

Jeremy Wallis, *Impressionists*. Chicago: Heinemann Library, 2003. Discusses the characteristics of the Impressionism movement, which began in the 1860s, and presents biographies of fourteen Impressionist artists.

Jude Welton, *Monet*. London: Dorling Kindersley, 2000. An informative guide by an art historian which tells the fascinating story of Monet's life and work. Photographs show the methods and materials Monet used to create his masterpieces, while the author offers a unique "eyewitness" view of the painter's distinctive canvases and the complex personality behind them.

Internet Source

Nicolas Pioch, "Monet, Claude," Web Museum, Paris, September 19, 2002. www.ibiblio.org/wm/paint/auth/

monet. A site with detailed information about the French Impressionist with links to reproductions and text concerning the artist's early works, first Impressionist paintings, Rouen Cathedral, water lilies, and more.

Web Sites

Classicartrepro: The Art of Monet (www.artofmonet.com/Home_Page.htm). A Web site with extensive documentation of Monet's work, with excellent reproductions representing all periods of the artist's career, including the gardens of Giverney, the series paintings, portraits, figure studies, and winter scenes.

The Monet Museum.com (www.monetmuseum.com/links.shtml). A site with links to more than a dozen Monet Web sites.

Musée Marmottan Monet (www.marmottan.com/uk). The Marmottan possesses the largest collection of Monet paintings in the world, and this Web site provides details about Monet as well as dozens of other Impressionists including Degas, Manet, Pissaro, and Renoir.

Welcome to Claude Monet's: Giverny and Vernon (http://giverny.org/monet/welcome.htm). The official Web site of Monet's home in Giverny, now a museum, with photo tours of his gardens, a biography, reproductions of his art, and links to articles about the colors he used and the Japanese woodblock art he collected.

Index

Picture Credits

Cover photo: © Bettmann/Corbis

Adoc-photos/Art Resource, NY, 21

AP Images, 9

© Bettmann/Corbis, 81 (bottom)

© Brooklyn Museum of Art, New York, USA/The Bridgeman Art Library, 90 (top)

Claude Monet, French, 1840-1926. *La Japonaise (Camille Monet in Japanese Costume)*, 1876. Oil on canvas. 231.8 x 142.3 cm (91 1/4 x 56 in.) Museum of Fine Arts, Boston. 1951 Purchase Fund, 56.147. Photograph © 2008 Museum of Fine Arts, Boston, 61

© Corbis, 25

Erich Lessing/Art Resource, NY, 36, 38, 47, 56, 64, 70, 83

Farrell Grehan/National Geographic/Getty Images, 88

Getty Images, 90 (bottom)

Image copyright © The Metropolitan Museum of Art/Art Resource, NY, 13, 40, 48, 53

© Kunsthalle, Bremen, Germany/ Lauros/ Giraudon/The Bridgeman Art Library, 29

The Library of Congress, 14

© Museum of Art, Santa Barbara, California, CA, USA/The Bridgeman Art Library, 75

© Neue Pinakothek, Munich, Germany/The Bridgeman Art Library, 52

The Philadelphia Museum of Art/Art Resource, NY, 93

© Private Collection/ © Agnew's, London, UK/The Bridgeman Art Library, 81 (top)

© Private Collection/Photo © Christie's Images/The Bridgeman Art Library, 33

Réunion des Musées Nationaux/Art Resource, NY, 65, 86, 94, 98–99

Roger Viollet/Getty Images, 73

Scala/Art Resource, NY, 26, 30

© Underwood & Underwood/Corbis, 17, 87

Yale University Art Gallery/Art Resource, NY, 43

About the Author

Stuart A. Kallen is the prolific author of more than 250 non-fiction books for children and young adults. He has written on topics ranging from the theory of relativity to the history of world music. In addition, Kallen has written award-winning children's videos and television scripts. In his spare time, he is a singer/songwriter/guitarist in San Diego, California.